Life has dealt me too many trials, heartbreak, and losses to count. But even while enduring suffering—God continued and continues to keep me. See, I've wanted to give up several times, but each time God said, *"Travasa, you're my child, and I will never leave you nor forsake you. I got you!"* I pray that no matter what you're dealing with, you know that God has you too.

So may each devotional you read be a divine blessing and encourage you daily. And even when the enemy whispers in your ear, *"Give up,"* tell him you're in it for the LONG HAUL.

Sincerely,
Travasa

THE
LONG
HAUL

THE LONG HAUL

TRAVASA HOLLOWAY

TNHB Inspirations
Rock Hill, South Carolina

THE LONG HAUL

Published by
TNHB Inspirations
Rock Hill, SC.
tnhb@tnhb-inspirations.com

Travasa Holloway, Publisher
Editorial Services TNHB Inspirations LLC
Yvonne Rose/Qualitypress.info – Book Packager

Copyright © 2023 Travasa Holloway
ISBN# 979-8-218-27034-6
Library of Congress Control Number: 2023917216

DEDICATION

I dedicate this writing journey to my handsome twin sons:

Ra'Mon aka Ray and Rod Holloway.

I am beyond proud of the men you have become,

and I am so honored to be your mother.

I love you Punkins!

ACKNOWLEDGEMENTS

With gratitude, I thank God for not taking His hands off me when I wanted to let go. I realize the gift that I have to encourage others, and I'm grateful for the angels that He has encompassed around me when I need an encouraging Word to get through my day. With Love, I thank you, and I love you to life.

Ra'Mon & Rod Holloway

The Holloway Ladies (Barbara, Brenda, Carla, Khara & Tekeye)

Pastor Rabon L. & Mia Turner (Grace Emmanuel Baptist Church of Flint MI)

Pastor Tyshawn & Shonetay Gardner (Tuscaloosa AL)

Dr. Derrol & Patricia H. Dawkins (New Start Covenant of Grace of Birmingham AL)

Pastor Leroy & Tina Caudle (Eagles Nest Cathedral International of Huntsville AL)

Bishop Daniel J. & Tiffany Richardson (Eagles Nest Cathedral International of Huntsville AL)

Sonya Drake (Huntsville AL)

Family & Friends

CONTENTS

INTRODUCTION

You win—you lose. Jobs start and end. Men and women come and go in relationships. But God is not like humans that He shall tell a lie or change His mind. His promises are His oath and are sacrosanct. Therefore, He will never leave nor forsake you. (Numbers 23:19) (Hebrews 6:18)

Life will have its challenges, and as easy as giving up seems like the answer, you can't! How do I know? I prayed. I waited, and I was highly frustrated. I even started to question everything. But at the end of the day, I kept my trust in God. I realized it was not my time—but His! (Isaiah 40:31)

I am Travasa Natasha Holloway of TNHB Inspirations

THE LONG HAUL

The race is not given to the swift nor to the strong.

But it is guaranteed to the one that endures to the end,

to the one that holds on for the LONG HAUL.

Regardless of what life directs and sends your way.

You must keep walking, for each step has been ordered by God.

So, keep walking, for it steadies your pace and, eventually,

navigates your way.

Knowing that every joy, sorrow, disappointment, trial,

your purpose, and even your dreams will all work together.

It will create a strength that you didn't realize that you
possessed.

So, keep walking as you heed the call.

One day you will be assured that it was good that you

hung on for the LONG HAUL.

Faint not; There's always a lesson right before the blessing.

-*Shannon Talley*

VoiceVessel Inspirations

AS YOU GROW, LET THEM GO

Have you ever felt like the more success and dreams you achieved others strayed away?

See, as God shifts you higher, expect to lose some people on the way. And that's okay because as you grow, they can't go.

Remember, your circle will get smaller as your visions become bigger.

"The righteous shall flourish like the palm tree: he shall grow like a cedar in Lebanon." (Psalm 92:12)

THE LONG HAUL

____

____

____

____

____

____

____

____

____

THE REAL DIET

How many of you have started the new year with a diet? See, there is nothing wrong with working on your appearance and looking your best. But if your relationship with Christ is not part of your regiment, then you're on the wrong diet. (John 6:27)

Remember, a healthy diet is with the word of God. (Matthew 5:6)

"O God, you are my God; earnestly I seek you; my soul thirsts for you; my flesh faints for you, as in a dry and weary land where there is no water." (Psalm 63:1)

THE LONG HAUL

A NEW YEAR, BUT AN OLD YOU

Are you a person that says, "This year is going to be different," but four days into the new year, you're back to the same thing as before?

See, last year is gone, but today is here. And you can continue to do what you did before or press forward with God in the new. (Philippians 3:14)

Remember, another new year won't mean anything if you're acting like the old you. (2 Corinthians 5:17)

"For I am about to do something new. See, I have already begun! Do you not see it?" (Isaiah 43:19)

THE LONG HAUL

____

____

____

____

____

____

____

THE SECRET

Have you ever been asked to keep a secret regarding something you're doing or in?

See, it's one thing to be a confidant and another to be in something that you KNOW God wouldn't approve of. (James 4:17)

Remember, if it must be kept a secret, you don't need to be in it.

"No temptation has overtaken you that is not common to man. God is faithful, and He will not let you be tempted beyond your ability, but with the temptation He will also provide the way of escape, that you may be able to endure it." (1 Corinthians 10:13)

THE LONG HAUL

THE THIEF

How would you feel if someone was to enter your home and steal things that belonged to you?

See, no one wants to be robbed of anything. But if you allow fear to enter your life, you're robbing yourself.

Remember, fear is a thief and will take your joy, peace, and dreams. Release it now. (2 Timothy 1:7)

"For you did not receive the spirit of slavery to fall back into fear, but you have received the Spirit of adoption as sons, by whom we cry, "Abba! Father!" (Romans 8:15)

THE LONG HAUL

HARD TO TAKE BACK

It's a common regret. (Blurting out something that you really didn't want to say.) Sound familiar?

See, what you say is like toothpaste being squeezed out of a tube. You can push and get it out. But you can't put it back in.

Remember, be careful with the words you speak aloud because you can't take them back. (Proverbs 29:20)

"Understand this, my dear brothers and sisters: You must all be quick to listen, slow to speak, and slow to get angry." (James 1:19)

THE LONG HAUL

DISCERN THE DOOR

Have you ever been in a situation where you're questioning if you should go in the door that's being opened to you?

See, more than ever now, discernment is necessary. Why? Because it is the gift from God that will help identify the way you should go—right from wrong and evil to good. (1 John 4:1) (Hebrews 5:14)

Remember, discern the doors before you walk through them.

"And it is my prayer that your love may abound more and more, with knowledge and all discernment, so that you may approve what is excellent, and so be pure and blameless for the day of Christ." (Philippians 1:9-10)

THE LONG HAUL

THE DUE DATE

Due dates are often thought of as when a pregnant woman gives birth. But not everyone is with a child, so the question is, what due date are you waiting for?

See, the date doesn't matter because God has a due season. And just because you want your delivery to take place on your time doesn't mean God will deliver it. (Galatians 6:9)

Remember, stop rushing Him, and trust Him. (Proverbs 3:5-6)

"This vision is for a future time. It describes the end, and it will be fulfilled. If it seems slow in coming, wait patiently, for it will surely take place. It will not be delayed." (Habakkuk 2:3)

THE LONG HAUL

LOVE FROM A DISTANCE

Let's face it; there are some people that you can keep in your heart, but the farther they are from you, the better.

See, it's not your job to try to change folks. And as much as you want better for them, they have to want it too.

Remember, sometimes the best thing you can do for them is love them from a distance.

"May the LORD keep watch between you and me when we are absent from each other." (Genesis 31:49)

THE LONG HAUL

ROTTEN FRUIT

It's the typical boomerang; they hurt you, and now you want to hurt them.

See, it's human nature to want to seek revenge. But the truth is, vengeance doesn't belong to you. (Romans 12:19)

Remember, you don't have to plot and plan how to deal with the corrupt. Rotten fruit will eventually fall. (Isaiah 8:15)

"So, I tried to understand why the wicked prosper. But what a difficult task it is! Then I went into your sanctuary, O God, and I finally understood the destiny of the wicked. Truly, you put them on a slippery path and send them sliding over the cliff to destruction." (Psalm 73:16-18)

THE LONG HAUL

DON'T LAY THERE

Let's face it; you're going to fall in life. Whether you get pushed or stumble, it's going to happen. So, the question is, how long will you stay down?

See, there is no shame in falling. But there is when you refuse to stand back up. (Proverbs 24:16)

Remember, don't beat yourself up for falling. Just make sure you don't lay there. (Psalm 37:24)

"They collapse and fall, but we rise and stand upright." (Psalm 20:8)

THE LONG HAUL

24 CARAT GOLD

A reputation is a generalized opinion or belief of what others think of you. But folks aren't the only ones with reputations.

See, God has a reputation too; and it's one that's twenty-four-carat gold with a lifetime guarantee. And based on that, you have every reason to trust Him. (Psalm 19:9-14)

Remember, God will not mess up His name on you. TRUST- He WILL come through. (Numbers 23:19)

"So, God has given both his promise and his oath. These two things are unchangeable because it is impossible for God to lie. Therefore, we who have fled to him for refuge can have great confidence as we hold to the hope that lies before us." (Hebrews 6:18)

THE LONG HAUL

____

____

____

____

____

____

____

BE RESPONSIBLE

When people hurt and do things to harm you, it's natural to want them to take ownership of the pain they caused. But what happens when they don't?

See, it doesn't matter what others do. But it does matter how you respond.

Remember, the responsibility of your pain is on them, but the healing is on you.

"Nevertheless, I will bring health and healing to it; I will heal my people and will let them enjoy abundant peace and security." (Jeremiah 33:6)

THE LONG HAUL

____

____

____

____

____

____

____

LOSING SLEEP

In bed, tossing and turning, and at the same time, staring at the ceiling. Why? Because you're worried about a problem that's out of your control anyway. Sound Familiar?

See, no matter the issue; God wants you to rest well. That's why you can lie down with ease because He sustains you. (Psalm 3:5)

Remember, while you're losing sleep over the one that did you wrong, they're sleeping like a baby. So, therefore, Let IT GO!

"I will lie down and sleep in peace, for You alone, O LORD, make me dwell in safety." (Psalm 4:8)

THE LONG HAUL

A SAD STORY

Let's face it; everyone has a sad story they can share that touches your heart. But the question is, how many times will you tell it?

There's a difference between giving your testimony and having a pity party.

Remember, if you're going to tell it, share the goodness of God in it. You're not a victim, but victorious. (1 Corinthians 15:57)

"No, in all these things we are more than conquerors through Him who loved us." (Romans 8:37)

THE LONG HAUL

A PUNISHED FUTURE

Carrying the past into your now only handcuffs you to it. The question is, does that describe you?

See, once you focus your energy on the past, you no longer live in the present moment.

Remember, don't punish your future based on past events. Now is here! (Isaiah 65:17)

"Forget the former things; do not dwell on the past. See, I am doing a new thing! Now it springs up; do you not perceive it? I am making a way in the wilderness and streams in the wasteland." (Isaiah 43:18-19)

THE LONG HAUL

YOU'RE A VESSEL FULL OF POWER

Life has a way of hitting you like a tsunami. And with everything becoming overwhelming, a question arises, how do I go on?

See, just like an action movie with a disaster, you're a star, and the enemy or your circumstances will never defeat you. (2 Corinthians 4:6-7)

Remember, you're a vessel full of power, and there is treasure inside you from the Lord that will get you through ANYTHING! (2 Corinthians 4)

"We are pressed on every side by troubles, but we are not crushed. We are perplexed, but not driven to despair. We are hunted down, but never abandoned by God. We get knocked down, but we are not destroyed." (2 Corinthians 4:8-9)

THE LONG HAUL

PATIENCE OR WASTED TIME?

Patience is something that isn't liked but is necessary. However, the question lies in knowing the difference between patiently waiting and wasting your time.

See, patience is a virtue and an excellent attribute to have. But that's why God requires discernment so that you can distinguish between the two. (Hebrews 5:14)

Remember, know when to have patience and when to let go.

"But examine everything carefully; hold fast to that which is good." (1 Thessalonians 5:21)

THE LONG HAUL

THE DECISION THAT BROKE YOUR HEART

When faced with a tough decision to make, it can be difficult. But not making one can have consequences.

See, sometimes you have to look out for yourself. And that means choosing YOU and your happiness even if someone else doesn't approve.

Remember, your decision might hurt your heart but bring you peace.

"To acquire wisdom is to love oneself; people who cherish understanding will prosper." (Proverbs 19:8)

THE LONG HAUL

____

____

____

____

____

____

____

____

POINT MADE

Let's face it; there's nothing wrong with an argument occasionally. But it's when it gets unhealthy that the problem lies.

See, there's a difference between having a good debate and having an ugly argument with someone. And at some point, you must decide; I'm shutting this down.

Remember, once your point is made, stop talking. (James 1:19)

"Better is the end of a thing than its beginning, and the patient in spirit is better than the proud in spirit." (Ecclesiastes 7:8)

THE LONG HAUL

THE TANTRUM

Do you know a child that throws a tantrum when they don't get their way? And before you think of a kid, are you one of them?

See, children aren't the only ones that can throw a fit. Grown adults *(Christians)* also throw spiritual hysterics while waiting on God to act.

Remember, your tantrums don't move God. So, stop whining and patiently wait on Him. (Isaiah 30:18)

"Dear brothers and sisters, don't be childish in your understanding of these things. Be innocent as babies when it comes to evil, but be mature in understanding matters of this kind." (1 Corinthians 14:20)

THE LONG HAUL

DEAD SITUATIONS

Have you ever tried to revive a dead situation? In other words, circumstances that no longer serve you.

See, folks are known to keep fighting for long-gone things. And although giving up is not something you should do, there are times when it is warranted. (Isaiah 43:18-19)

Remember, stop breathing life into things that are weighing you down. It's dead, so let it go!

"A time to search and a time to give up as lost; A time to keep and a time to throw away." (Ecclesiastes 3:6)

THE LONG HAUL

I REMEMBER WHEN...

It's one thing to know who your enemy is and how you will take action in dealing with them. But what happens when you're the enemy?

See, all memories aren't good. And if yours is constantly bringing up things from that past that you need to release, then YOU are your bandit.

Remember, your adversary is often your memory. And if you don't let it go, it will halt your future.

"Behold, I am creating new heavens and a new earth; And the former things [of life] will not be remembered or come to mind." (Isaiah 65:17)

THE LONG HAUL

____

____

____

____

____

____

____

____

A PLATE OF HARDSHIPS

Sometimes, life can serve you a plate of hardships: trials, suffering, and adversaries.

See, your problems may be there, but they're not permanent. And although it feels as if it's breaking you, it should catapult you to God instead. (Psalm 107:28-31)

Remember, God is the one that turns night into day. Therefore, He will turn your burdens into blessings. (Amos 5:8)

"Jesus responded, 'Why are you afraid? You have so little faith!' Then he got up and rebuked the wind and waves, and suddenly there was a great calm." (Matthew 8:26)

THE LONG HAUL

NO DRAMA PLEASE

It's a statement constantly being shouted, posted, and said aloud, "No Drama Please."

See, in life, there will be dramatic events that will occur. But there's a difference between walking into it and creating turmoil.

Remember, without participation, drama can't survive.

"Where *there is* no wood, the fire goes out; And where *there is* no talebearer, strife ceases." (Proverbs 26:20)

THE LONG HAUL

SYMPATHY OR STRENGTH

Have you ever been through something and just had to get the frustration off your chest?

See, it's okay to let off some steam every once in a while. But there's a difference between venting and showcasing yourself as a victim.

Remember, before you tell your business, ask one question: Do I need sympathy or strength? (Proverbs 13:3)

"Seek out the LORD and His strength; seek His face always." (1 Chronicles 16:11)

THE LONG HAUL

FAITH HELPER

L et's face it; there will be times when life seems overwhelming. And if you don't keep your eyes on the Lord, your faith might wither. (Hebrews 12:2)

See, it can be strenuous to maintain faith during difficult times. And although it looks like there's no hope, that's when your faith should increase the most. (Hebrews 11:1)

Remember, even if your faith is weak, you always have a faith helper in God. (1 John 5:4)

"So faith comes from hearing, and hearing through the word of Christ." (Romans 10:17)

THE LONG HAUL

PASS THE BATON

A relay race is a track and field event where athletes run at a set distance carrying a baton before passing to the next runner to go the distance. The question is: How are you running your race?

See, you might not be a physical athlete, but it's your job and responsibility to pass the knowledge of Christ to the next. In other words, your story is that testimony to help the next person. (Revelation 12:11)

Remember, pass the baton, and testify to what Christ has done for you and how He can do the same for them. (Luke 8:39)

"Therefore, do not be ashamed of the testimony about our Lord, nor of me, his prisoner; but share in suffering for the gospel by the power of God." (2 Timothy 1:8)

THE LONG HAUL

THE EXPRESSION OF REGRET

How many of you are waiting for an apology? But if you are honest with yourself, you know it isn't coming. (Ephesians 4:32)

See, you must learn to be okay with the "sorry" you will never get. *Why?* Because folks don't owe you anything. Your job is to forgive, give it to God, and move on. (1 Peter 5:7) (Mark 11:25)

So, get up and stop waiting for the *expression of regret*—it isn't going to happen. The hurt and disrespect you encountered was the closure! (Philippians 4:6-7) (Judges 11:27)

"May the LORD judge between you and me. And may the LORD avenge the wrongs you have done to me, but my hand will not touch you." (1 Samuel 24:12)

THE LONG HAUL

____

____

____

____

____

____

____

THE UNSUPPORTIVE PEOPLE

Have you ever had something fantastic happen to you? And the people (family/friends) you thought would be the first to clap didn't say anything at all.

See, those people are called unsupportive. And although it might hurt because they aren't showing the support you deserve, the lack of it still won't stop your shine.

Remember, don't worry about the ones that won't support you. God will send others (strangers, i.e., angels) to be your support system.

"The LORD will send a blessing on your barns and on everything you put your hand to. The LORD your God will bless you in the land he is giving you." (Deuteronomy 2:8)

THE LONG HAUL

A SMALL MISUNDERSTANDING

Let's face it; misunderstandings happen more often than we like to admit. Whether you misheard something that was said, or your words were misunderstood. The fact is, they occur.

See, regardless of the misinterpretation; nothing warrants hatefulness. That means if the person pops, snaps, and goes off, they just showed you who they are.

Remember, God will always reveal folks' character and intentions after a small misunderstanding.

"As a prisoner for the Lord, then, I urge you to live a life worthy of the calling you have received. Be completely humble and gentle; be patient, bearing with one another in love. Make every effort to keep the unity of the Spirit through the bond of peace." (Ephesians 4:1-3)

THE LONG HAUL

DUCK & RUN

The enemy comes to steal, kill, and destroy you from the North, South, East, and West. The question is, what do you do about it? (John 10:10)

See, it can't be your reaction to duck and run; but that's what the enemy wants you to do. He's cunning in his strategy, but God gives you everything you need to resist and defeat his schemes and plots. (Ephesians 6:10-12)

Remember, you're a child of God, so stand firm and be unmovable. (1 Corinthians 15:58)

"The LORD will cause your enemies who rise against you to be defeated before you. They shall come out against you one way and flee before you seven ways." (Deuteronomy 28:7)

THE LONG HAUL

THE INVITATION

Let's face it; somebody somewhere right now is going through something. So, the question is, are you that person?

See, problems are going to arise, no matter who you are. But it's how you handle them that matters. (Philippians 4:6-7)

Remember, problems are your invitation to prayer.

"I have told you all this so that you may have peace in me. Here on earth, you will have many trials and sorrows. But take heart, because I have overcome the world." (John 16:33)

THE LONG HAUL

NOT MY FRIEND

Nowadays, folks are quick to say they have many friends. But the fact is, it's not quantity but quality.

See, you can have someone close to you that is indeed your friend. But just because they have other acquaintances doesn't make you close to them.

Remember, sometimes you have to remind your friend that their friend shouldn't know your business. (Proverbs 27:6)

"A troublemaker plants seeds of strife; gossip separates the best of friends." (Proverbs 16:28)

THE LONG HAUL

HAND IT OVER

Have you ever magnified a problem so much that you thought that it has become too big for God too?

See, there's nothing you're going through that's too hard for God. Now, it might overwhelm you, but that's why you give it to Him. (Luke 18:27) (1 Peter 5:7)

Remember, if it's a big enough problem for you to be worried about, it's big enough for you to hand over. (Isaiah 41:10)

"Oh, Lord GOD! You have made the heavens and the earth by Your great power and outstretched arm. Nothing is too difficult for You!" (Jeremiah 32:17)

THE LONG HAUL

LOOK WHAT I'M GIVING UP

Being comfortable feels good, right? So why give up your comfort for the unknown?

See, as much as you're scared to take the leap of faith for change. You must do it because you will never know what God has in store for you if you don't. (Ephesians 3:20) (Joshua 1:9)

Remember, stop focusing on what you're giving up and focus on what you have to gain. (Isaiah 43:18-19)

"For behold, I will create new heavens and a new earth. The former things will not be remembered, nor will they come to mind." (Isaiah 65:17)

THE LONG HAUL

THE PERFORMING CLOWN

Some folks will do anything to become someone else. But if you're always chasing another's identity, when are you authentically you? (Psalm 139:14-16)

See, the fact is you can portray whomever you want. But just because your environment changes, it doesn't mean you do.

Remember, clowns can perform in a palace; that doesn't make them queens and kings; it just makes the castle a circus. (Ephesians 5:1)

"Dear friend, do not imitate what is evil but what is good. Anyone who does what is good is from God. Anyone who does what is evil has not seen God." (3 John 1:11)

THE LONG HAUL

FALLEN ON YOUR KNEES

Let's face it; when you're down to the point that all you can do is fall to your knees, you're in a good place.

See, as painful as trials and sorrows are, you're not in them alone. God is waiting and wanting you to bring Him your troubles. (Psalm 55:22)

Remember, once you've fallen to your knees, the battle isn't over; it's just getting started. (1 John 5:14-15)

"This is what the LORD says: Do not be afraid! Don't be discouraged by this mighty army, for the battle is not yours, but God's." (2 Chronicles 20:15)

THE LONG HAUL

CHECK YOUR RESPONSE

Have you ever wanted to explode because someone said or did something to set you off?

See, it's a natural reaction to want to use the same temperature they used on you to throw back on them. The reality is that you can't control how others treat you. But you can control how you respond to it.

Remember, the responsibility is on you in how you react with others. (Ephesians 4:32)

"Whoever is slow to anger has great understanding, but he who has a hasty temper exalts folly." (Proverbs 14:29)

THE LONG HAUL

TIMING IS EVERYTHING

Whether your patience doesn't want you to admit it or not, God is never early, never late, but always on time. (Psalm 27:13-14)

I get it; it will feel like an eternity when you must wait for God. But the fact is you have to wait, and your waiting isn't in vain. (Isaiah 40:31)

Remember, timing is everything. And at the right time, God will provide. (Ecclesiastes 3:1 & 8:6)

"Therefore, the Lord waits to be gracious to you, and therefore he exalts himself to show mercy to you. For the Lord is a God of justice; blessed are all those who wait for Him." (Isaiah 30:18)

THE LONG HAUL

PRAY OR TALK

Marcus Aurelius says it best, "How much time he gains who does not look to see what his neighbor says or does or thinks, but only at what he does himself." (Matthew 7:1-5)

See, it's easy to look at someone else and call out all their mistakes and be judgmental. But what does that say about you? (James 4:11-12)

Remember, if you don't pray for them, don't talk about them. (1 Timothy 2:1)

"Since you judge others for doing these things, why do you think you can avoid God's judgment when you do the same things?" (Romans 2:3)

THE LONG HAUL

FREE AT LAST

How many times have you cried, prayed, and even begged for God to intervene? And when He did, you repeated the cycle all over again.

See, there comes a time that YOU have to step up and do the work as well. And if you don't, you will continue to be like a dog that returns to his own vomit. (James 2:17) (Proverbs 26:11)

Remember, if you really want to be free, stop running back to what you asked God to deliver you from. (Romans 6:22)

"Sin is no longer your master, for you no longer live under the requirements of the law. Instead, you live under the freedom of God's grace." (Romans 6:14)

THE LONG HAUL

THE PAST ISN'T IDENTITY

Painful life experiences hurt. Whether you caused them or someone else, how you move forward afterward makes a difference.

See, the past is over with. In other words, you don't live there anymore, and you don't have to hold yourself hostage to the mistakes from it.

Remember, your past is your testimony. Never let it be your identity. (1 Peter 2:9) (Galatians 2:20)

"Therefore, if anyone is in Christ, he is a new creation. The old has passed away. Behold, the new has come!" (2 Corinthians 5:17)

THE LONG HAUL

ROUGH SEAS

Let's face it; not all rides are smooth sailing. And even when it gets rough, guess what? You still make it to your destination.

See, there will be times when life will get rocky. But it's okay because no matter how bumpy the ride is, YOU have God as your Captain. (Deuteronomy 31:6)

Remember, your destination won't change because the seas get rough. (Psalm 107:29)

"You rule the raging sea; when its waves mount up, You still them." (Psalm 89:9)

THE LONG HAUL

SURPRISE

Who doesn't like a surprise occasionally? Especially the ones when you receive an unexpected blessing/gift from it.

See, the truth is not everyone wants to be surprised. Why? Because surprises showcase that YOU aren't in control. (Matthew 6:34)

Remember, don't let the surprise get to you. Just let it go and give it to God. (Psalm 55:22)

"Dear friends, do not be surprised at the fiery ordeal that has come on you to test you, as though something strange were happening to you. But rejoice inasmuch as you participate in the sufferings of Christ, so that you may be overjoyed when his glory is revealed." (1 Peter 4:12-13)

THE LONG HAUL

THE STRUGGLE

Struggle—who wants to deal with it? But where would you be without it? (2 Timothy 2:12)

See, it's easy to detest what you think is making you weak; in actuality, it's building you. (Philippians 4:13)

Remember, it's not about the struggle; but about putting your faith in God, who gives you the strength to endure. (Romans 5:3-5)

"For you have need of endurance, so that when you have done the will of God you may receive what is promised." (Hebrews 10:36)

THE LONG HAUL

DOUBT OR TRUST

When you have no idea what will happen in your circumstances, it's easy to doubt, but just because you can do it doesn't mean you should. (Philippians 4:6)

Yes, I know it's scary, and you have no idea how God is going to bring you through. But the fact is, He will. YOU just have to trust Him. (Proverbs 3:5)

Remember, you can choose to have doubt and worry or trust in the Lord. (Psalm 37:4-6)

"The Lord is my strength and my shield; in Him my heart trusts, and I am helped; my heart exults, and with my song I give thanks to Him." (Psalm 28:7)

THE LONG HAUL

MY HANDS HURT

Doors close and open all the time. But you must know the ones you need to keep permanently closed. (1 John 4:1)

See, doors can signify your life in stages. In other words, sometimes the "door" will represent a relationship, job, or friendship that's done. But if you don't realize that, you will stand there yelling and banging, trying to get it back opened. (Philippians 1:9-10)

Remember, your hands will continue to hurt if you keep using a crowbar to open what God needs you to keep closed. (Jeremiah 29:11)

"The Lord will keep you from all harm- he will watch over your life; the Lord will watch over your coming and going, both now and forevermore." (Psalm 121:7-8)

THE LONG HAUL

IT'S SHOWTIME

Let's face it; there will come a time when you will receive bad news. And no matter what it is, you have to decide whether or not you will believe the enemy's report or God's. (Proverbs 3:5)

See, as much as you want to fall out on the floor kicking and screaming, that's exactly what you shouldn't do. Instead, you need to wipe your face, lift your head, and show the world that you are more than a conqueror. (Romans 8:31-39) (Philippians 4:13)

Remember, it's showtime. So, show you're still standing, you're still here, and everything the enemy meant for evil, God is working for your good. (Genesis 50:20)

"Strengthened with all might, according to His glorious power, for all patience and longsuffering with joy." (Colossians 1:11)

THE LONG HAUL

DO NOT PROCEED

If you're a driver, you've come upon a roadblock. And if you have never driven, think about the times you faced an obstacle trying to accomplish something.

See, as much as folks don't want anything to block what they're trying to do. All roadblocks aren't a bad thing.

Remember, just because you want to move forward, God sometimes says, *"Do Not Proceed."* Why? Because you only see what's in front of you, but He sees the entire road. (Hosea 2:6) (Lamentations 3:7-9)

"God has blocked my way so I cannot move. He has plunged my path into darkness." (Job 19:8)

THE LONG HAUL

WHEN THEY KNOCK YOU DOWN

Let's face it; some folks will knock or push you down. So, the question is, what do you do after you get up, or do you even get up at all?

See, if someone is the reason you fall, that's on them. But the responsibility is on you whether you get back up.

Remember, if you get knocked down, don't make a wrong decision by running back to who or what threw you there in the first place. (Proverbs 26:11)

"Rejoice not over me, O my enemy; when I fall, I shall rise; when I sit in darkness, the LORD will be a light to me." (Micah 7:8)

THE LONG HAUL

DUPLICATING THE PAST

How many of you have made mistakes? Now how many of you have learned from them?

See, everyone will mess up from time to time. But if you keep repeating what you did, it' becomes your habit. (Proverbs 26:11)

Remember, it's a new day, so you don't have to duplicate the mistakes from the past. (Psalm 118:24)

"Dear friends, if we deliberately continue sinning after we have received knowledge of the truth, there is no longer any sacrifice that will cover these sins. "There is only the terrible expectation of God's judgment and the raging fire that will consume his enemies." (Hebrews 10:26-27)

THE LONG HAUL

____

____

____

____

____

____

____

HIGHER THE LEVEL BIGGER THE DEVIL

Have you ever heard: *"Higher The Level Bigger The Devil?"* See, once you receive God's blessings for you, expect attacks. Why? Because the more you get to God's destiny for your life, demons come on assignment for you. (Ephesians 6-11-18)

Remember, with promotion comes intimidation. Proceed anyway. The Lord is with YOU! (Deuteronomy 31:6)

"So do not fear, for I am with you; do not be dismayed, for I am your God. I will strengthen you and help you; I will uphold you with my righteous right hand." (Isiah 40:10)

THE LONG HAUL

THE SHOES YOU WEAR

There's nothing wrong with wanting and having nice things and wearing them. But the problem lies when you get caught up on what's outside instead of the inside.

See, you can look at someone's outer appearance and think they have it all together. When in actuality, the inside is rotten to the core. (1 Samuel 16:7)

Remember, destiny isn't determined by what you're wearing or the shoes you have. But by the steps you are taking.

"Keep steady my steps according to your promise, and let no iniquity get dominion over me." (Psalm 119:133)

THE LONG HAUL

YOUR SECRET

How many of you are doing something you know you shouldn't do?

See, no matter your guilty pleasure, all sins have consequences. And you can't blame others when you knowingly continue to do what will cost you.

Remember, if what you're doing has to be a kept secret— it's time to stop!

"Anyone, then, who knows the right thing to do, yet fails to do it, is guilty of sin." (James 4:17)

THE LONG HAUL

COMPRISING YOUR SANITY

Peace is a wonderful thing. But only some people have it. See, there should be nothing you're doing or in that should comprise your sanity or peace. And if you are, it's time to do something about it.

Remember, nothing should be so expensive that it costs you peace of mind. (Romans 16:20)

"May the God of hope fill you with all joy and peace in believing, so that by the power of the Holy Spirit you may abound in hope." (Romans 15:13)

THE LONG HAUL

CLAP FOR THEM

Have you ever tried to do something, but a loved one or friend beat you to it?

See, life isn't a speed race. And if your neighbor happens to get there before you, it's okay. You're running your race, not theirs.

Remember, clap for people who are ahead of you. Your time is coming!

"But as for you, be strong and do not give up, for your work will be rewarded." (2 Chronicles 15:7)

THE LONG HAUL

THE PROBLEM IS YOU

How many of you have a problem or situation that you're in that feels hopeless?

See, God protected David from Goliath. Daniel, in the lion's den, covered Shadrach, Meshach, and Abednego in the fiery furnace. So, what makes you think He won't help you? (1 Samuel 17:1-58) (Daniel 6:12-28) (Daniel 3:16-28)

Remember, the problem isn't God. It's YOU! Why? Because you have a faith problem, and your faith must trump what you see. (Hebrews 11:1)

"And without faith it is impossible to please *Him,* for the one who comes to God must believe that He exists, and *that* He proves to be One who rewards those who seek Him." (Hebrews 11:6)

THE LONG HAUL

SMALL STEPS

Are you frustrated because you're not where you want to be yet? See, it's a good thing to have goals. But you still have to give yourself applause for even trying. And your baby steps have power in them.

Remember, don't underestimate the work you're doing. Small steps are bigger than no steps.

"But as for you, be strong and do not give up, for your work will be rewarded." (2 Chronicles 15:7)

THE LONG HAUL

THE UNSEATED

Have you ever sat down somewhere but felt like others didn't want you there? (Psalm 23:5)

See, folks don't have the power to make you leave where God has placed you. So, no matter what they think, you're where you're supposed to be. (Psalm 75:6-7)

Remember, if God has prepared you there, NO ONE can unseat you! (Revelation 3:7)

"I know your deeds. See, I have placed before you an open door that no one can shut. I know that you have little strength, yet you have kept my word and have not denied my name." (Revelation 3:8)

THE LONG HAUL

THE ENEMY'S SHENANIGANS

Whether it's the roaring lion or the sneaky serpent, one thing is for sure; the enemy comes for you. The question is, "Are you prepared to deal with it?" (Ephesians 6:11-13)

See, once you focus on the enemy instead of God, you open the door to his distractions. And your eyes turn on him instead of God. (Hebrews 12:2)

Remember, STAY FOCUSED. Keep your eyes on God and Him ONLY! (James 4:7)

"You will keep in perfect peace all who trust in you, all whose thoughts are fixed on you!" (Isaiah 26:3)

THE LONG HAUL

THE AUTOMATIC RESPONSE

It's the automatic response. *"They hurt you, and now you try to hurt them."* But the question is, what does that solve? (Proverbs 20:22)

I get it. You want to feel better, and better often looks like hitting them where they hurt you. But the fact is, vengeance isn't yours to handle. (Deuteronomy 32:35)

Remember, the best revenge is none. So, stop seeking retribution. Heal and move on. (Romans 12:17-19)

"Do not say, 'I'll pay you back for this wrong!' Wait for the LORD, and He will avenge you." (Proverbs 20:22)

THE LONG HAUL

A BIG PROBLEM

Problems are something that none of us want. But we all have. (James 1:2)

See, the situation you're in could be big. But the fact is, God is bigger. And He can handle whatever you bring. (Jeremiah 32:27)

Remember, whatever is weighing you down, give it to God. For there is nothing in your life you're going through that is impossible for Him. (Luke 1:37)

"Jesus looked at them and said, 'With man this is impossible, but with God all things are possible.'" (Matthew 19:26)

THE LONG HAUL

THEY KNOW EVERYTHING

Some folks feel that the more you learn, the better you'll become. But let's face it; others are Know It-All's. (Proverbs 13:16)

See, it's a lack of awareness when you think you can't be taught. The greatest enemy of knowledge is not ignorance. It is an illusion of knowledge. (Stephen Hawkins) (Proverbs 18:15)

Remember, you can't help people who already know everything. (Proverbs 1:7)

"The wise don't make a show of their knowledge, but fools broadcast their foolishness." (Proverbs 12:23)

THE LONG HAUL

A LIFE OF CHAOS

Do you know what it's like to have a life full of confusion? (1 Peter 5:8)

See, God is peace and harmony. And if your life is a season of chaos, it's time to do something about it. (1 Corinthians 7:15)

So, what do you do? You allow the Holy Spirit to help guide you to believe God's truth over any lies and confusion you're in. (John 16:13)

"For God is not a God of confusion but of peace." (1 Corinthians 13:33)

THE LONG HAUL

KNOCK KNOCK, COME IN

When people knock on your door, do you always let them in? (Philippians 1:9-10)

See, just like your home; your space is sacrosanct. And not everyone trying to come in has good intentions. (Matthew 7:15)

Remember, be careful of the people you grant access to. Some are coming to destroy you. (1 Peter 5:8)

"Dear friends, do not believe every spirit, but test the spirits to see whether they are from God, because many false prophets have gone out into the world." (1 John 4:1)

THE LONG HAUL

THE ENEMY OR YOUR CONSEQUENCE?

When folks think the enemy is the cause of their problems, it's easy to throw the blame. But the fact is, everything isn't the enemy. (John 10:10)

See, attacks are caused when the enemy keeps you from God's will. But your consequence is a result of when YOU ignore the will of God. (Romans 1:18-32)

Remember, not all things that happen to you are the enemy at work. Sometimes, it's YOU. (Proverbs 1:24-33)

"When pride comes, disgrace follows, but with humility comes wisdom." (Proverbs 11:2)

THE LONG HAUL

NO LIGHT

Let's face it; there are times when life gets dark. And no matter how hard you try to see the light, things seem to get darker. (Psalm 27:1)

See, the truth is that there is light at the end of the tunnel. However, for you to see it, you must move forward. (Psalm 119:105)

Remember, don't stop moving when it seems dark. Turn to God, who is your Light, and He will see you through! (John 1:5)

"Again, Jesus spoke to them, saying, "I am the light of the world. Whoever follows me will not walk in darkness, but will have the light of life." (John 8:12)

THE LONG HAUL

A CHICKEN WITH THEIR HEAD CUT OFF

When bad news hits, do you begin to panic or pray? (1 Kings 8:28)

See, as easy as it is to say you pray, be honest with yourself. Because if you're running around like a chicken with your head cut off telling everyone what's wrong, well, you're in full panic mode. (Philippians 4:6-7)

Remember, calm down, stop worrying, and begin to worship. So, take a deep breath, pause, and reset. Now give it to God! (1 Peter 5:7)

"Let not your hearts be troubled. Believe in God; believe also in me." (John 12:1)

THE LONG HAUL

GOD'S SCHEDULE

When you have to wait on God, it can be challenging. But not waiting on Him can have consequences. (Isaiah 40:28-31)

See, no matter what hissy fit you throw; God will still do it in HIS TIME. And if you choose to disobey it, the repercussion will be on YOU. (Luke 6:46) (James 1:14-15)

So, ask yourself: "Do you want your time or God's Schedule?" (2 Peter 3:8)

He said to them: "It is not for you to know the times or dates the Father has set by his own authority." (Acts 1:7)

THE LONG HAUL

____

____

____

____

____

____

____

____

YOUR RESPONSE IS CRITICAL

When someone says something you don't like, what's your response? (Proverbs 15:1)

See, just because you can pop, jump, and go off, that doesn't mean you should. Why? Because your reply is critical to any conflict. (Ephesians 4:29)

Remember, your response is your responsibility. So, it will be on YOU if you lose any opportunity with the wrong response. (Proverbs 12:18; 18:21)

"I tell you, on the day of judgment people will give account for every careless word they speak." (Matthew 12:36)

THE LONG HAUL

____

____

____

____

____

____

____

____

RAIN GROWS FLOWERS

When you're in an argument or a heated debate, do you find yourself yelling, trying to get your point across? (Ephesians 4:29)

I get it—you're passionate about what you're trying to say. But a raised voice is nothing but a sword thrusting at whom you're speaking to. And when you're swinging, the other person goes on the defense and won't hear your words. (James 3:6)

Remember, let your words be sweet like a honeycomb. It's rain that grows flowers, not thunder! (Proverbs 16:24)

"But now you must also rid yourselves of all such things as these: anger, rage, malice, slander, and filthy language from your lips." (Colossians 3:8)

THE LONG HAUL

THE ENEMY NEXT TO YOU

How many of you know your enemy? (1 Peter 5:8) See, it's one thing when you can recognize who your opponent is. But the truth is, sometimes your enemy is right next to you. (Psalm 41:9)

Remember, be careful of everyone you call a friend and those you tell everything to. Why? Because you might just be educating the enemy. (Jeremiah 9:4)

"Enemies disguise themselves with their lips, but in their hearts, they harbor deceit." (Proverbs 26:24)

THE LONG HAUL

CLOSE YOUR EARS

Satan started with his lies and destruction at the very beginning of creation. And even now, today, he's more cunning and smart. The question is, how do you handle him? (2 Corinthians 11:3)

See, because Satan is a liar and tries to throw you off course. That doesn't mean you have to listen. (John 8:44)

Remember, Satan is a deceiver. So, close your ears and never listen to a word he tries to tell you. (Ephesians 6:11)

"Stay alert! Watch out for your great enemy, the devil. He prowls around like a roaring lion, looking for someone to devour." (1 Peter 5:8)

THE LONG HAUL

I CAN'T FORGET ABOUT IT

Have you ever had something happen to you that you couldn't seem to shake? (2 Corinthians 5:17)

See, bad things are going to occur. That's a fact. But just because they happen doesn't mean you have to stop living. (Philippians 3:13-14)

Remember, when you stay stuck on what transpired, you'll never see what God has in store. (Isaiah 43:18-19)

"You intended to harm me, but God intended it all for good." (Genesis 50:20)

THE LONG HAUL

JUSTIFYING THE KNIFE

It's one thing to have scars that weren't by your doing. But how many marks do you have from giving the person who cut you with the knife? (1 Peter 5:8)

See, love doesn't delight in evil. And as much as you love someone, you still can't make an excuse for them when they cause you harm. (1 Corinthians 13:4-8)

Remember, stop justifying the knife that's causing you to bleed. (Jude 1:4)

"The Lord tests the righteous, but his soul hates the wicked and the one who loves violence." (Psalm 11:5)

THE LONG HAUL

SOMEONE SOMEWHERE

It's easy to look at someone else and think they have it made. But the truth is you don't know what they've been through to get to where they are. (Proverbs 14:30)

See, many folks see others NOW, but they have no idea about their THEN. So, instead of being envious, be grateful for all you have. (1 Thessalonians 5:18)

Remember, there is someone somewhere right now wishing for what you're taking for granted. (Psalm 118:1-18)

"Giving thanks always and for everything to God the Father in the name of our Lord Jesus Christ." (Ephesians 5:20)

THE LONG HAUL

A BAD YESTERDAY

How many of you have had a bad day? If I had to guess, that would be all of us. (2 Corinthians 5:17)

See, bad days are going to happen. That's a fact. But one bad day shouldn't make you go into the next with a bad attitude. (Proverbs 17:22)

Remember, don't ruin your today because of a bad yesterday. (Isaiah 43:18-19)

"This is the day the LORD has made. We will rejoice and be glad in it." (Psalm 118:24)

THE LONG HAUL

A CLUTTER MIND

Clutter is nothing more than an excessive amount of stuff crowding your space. But homes, offices, and cars aren't the only cluttered things. (Ecclesiastes 3:6)

When you have emotional baggage, you keep hauling around; it will affect your mind, body, soul, and spirit. And if you don't let it go, it will weigh you down. (Psalm 51:10)

Remember, stop letting the unnecessary clutter your mind. Be free—LET IT GO!

"For to be carnally minded *is* death; but to be spiritually minded *is* life and peace." (Romans 8:6)

THE LONG HAUL

NOSES UP IN THE AIR

Are you quick to judge and look down on others different from you? (Luke 6:37)

See, no one, and I mean absolutely nobody has the right to belittle another person. Why? Because you'll be speaking on someone who is sinning differently from you. (Matthew 7:1-5)

Remember, stop sticking your nose up in the air when you haven't even looked in the mirror. (Romans 2:3)

"There is only one lawgiver and judge, he who is able to save and to destroy. But who are you to judge your neighbor?" (James 4:12)

THE LONG HAUL

PLACED BY INTENT

Let's face it; no one wants to have a wicked person around them. But the truth is, they're there for a reason. (Romans 8:28)

See, when anything bad happens, and a person is the root of it, the question comes up of why. But God doesn't make mistakes. So, the enemy that's encamping around you is there by intent. (Jeremiah 29:11)

Remember, even Judas had a purpose. Trust and believe that God uses all things and people for your good! (John 13:21-27)

"You intended to harm me, but God intended it all for good." (Genesis 50:20)

THE LONG HAUL

CONTAGIOUS ATTITUDES

Are you cautious about spreading germs and common cold viruses to ensure others don't catch them? If so, are you the same about your attitude? (Leviticus 15:13)

See, if you're mindful about others becoming sick, the same practice should apply to your attitude. (Galatians 5:22-23)

Remember, your attitude is contagious, especially negative ones. So be careful not to contaminate those around you with your negativity. (Ecclesiastes 10:12)

"Let no corrupting talk come out of your mouths, but only such as is good for building up, as fits the occasion, that it may give grace to those who hear." (Ephesians 4:29)

THE LONG HAUL

THE HOLD

Lies, plots, schemes, and plans. These are all the enemy's strategies when he tries to hold you back and take you out. But God will use those same tactics to catapult you forward. (John 10:10) (Genesis 50:20)

See, the enemy can do whatever he wants. In other words, the weapon can form, but it won't prosper. (Isaiah 54:17)

Remember, not even the devil in hell can stop what God has in store for you. (Jeremiah 29:11)

"The God of peace will soon crush Satan under your feet. The grace of our Lord Jesus Christ be with you." (Romans 16:20)

THE LONG HAUL

____

____

____

____

____

____

____

THE UN'S

You've experienced the "un's" at some point in life. You know, unfair, unwanted, and unhappy. (James 1:2)

See, it doesn't matter what the unexpected, unknown, or unseen is. Because God will see you through all of it. (Isaiah 43:2)

Remember, the only "un's" you should focus on is being unstoppable. YOU got this! (Philippians 4:11-13) (1 Corinthians 2:5)

"Behold, I am with you and will keep you wherever you go, and will bring you back to this land. For I will not leave you until I have done what I have promised you." (Genesis 28:15)

THE LONG HAUL

____

____

____

____

____

____

____

____

BUT I NEED

No one wants to be in dire need, especially when their need is immediate. But the question is, who are you turning to? (James 4:8)

See, it's easy to call on family, loved ones, and friends for help. But you will be disappointed anytime you expect other people to meet your desires, instead of God. (Matthew 19:26)

Remember, whatever you need, turn to God. (Matthew 6:32) (2 Samuel 22:7)

"And my God shall supply all your need according to His riches in glory by Christ Jesus." (Philippians 4:19)

THE LONG HAUL

HIS GREATNESS NOT YOUR CIRCUMSTANCES

It's easy to praise God when things are all good. But are you still praising Him in the darkest of times? (James 5:13)

See, it's simple. No matter what season you're in, you should always praise God. Why? Because you should never let your emotions make you forget God's amazing love for you. (Psalm 100:4-5)

Remember, praise God according to His Greatness, not your circumstances. (Hebrews 13:15)

"The Lord is my strength and my song, and He has become my salvation; this is my God, and I will praise Him, my father's God, and I will exalt Him." (Exodus 15:2)

THE LONG HAUL

A FACT

Facts are actual things, and when you're going through a hard time or the biggest struggle of your life, that's a fact. But it's also a fact that God's Word is true! (Proverbs 30:5) (2 Samuel 22:31)

Yes, things might be bad, and you don't know what to do. But it's at that time you turn to God, who is your rock, fortress, and deliverer. (Psalm 18:2)

Remember, your condition is a fact, but God's word is the truth and will always change the facts! (John 17:17)

"Every word of God proves true; He is a shield to those who take refuge in Him." (Proverbs 30:5)

THE LONG HAUL

THE BETRAYAL

No one wants to be betrayed. But let's face it; treacherous, deceiving folks come into your life and stab you straight in the back. (Ephesians 6:10-18)

See, Jesus knows betrayal more than anybody. And because He knows what it feels like, He can help you through it. (John 13:18-30) (Matthew 26:23–25)

Remember, betrayal is often the best friend your destiny ever had! (Jeremiah 29:11)

"You intended to harm me, but God intended it all for good." (Genesis 50:20)

THE LONG HAUL

THE JOKE'S ON THEM

The enemy will play mind games and tricks to keep you off track and destroy you. But guess what? The joke is on them. (Psalm 21:11)

See, the enemy wants to get you to go in the opposite direction of God. So that means he will lie, scheme, and devise plans to keep you off course. This is why you have to put on God's whole armor to protect yourself from any devious plans he plots. (John 10:10) (Ephesians 6:10-18)

Remember, they might try to stop you; but no weapon formed against you will succeed. (Isaiah 54:17)

"May the evil plans of my enemies be turned against them. Do as you promised and put an end to them." (Psalm 54:5)

THE LONG HAUL

____

____

____

____

____

____

____

INSIDE OF YOU

Folks hit piñatas, rob banks, and break into houses. Why? Because of what's inside of them. (Lamentations 4:2)

See, you're no different. There is a special treasure inside of you. And the enemy wants it. But God has given you power and authority to overcome the enemy, and nothing he does will harm you. (2 Corinthians 4:7) (Luke 10:19)

Remember, you're valuable. That's why the attack is happening. The enemy wants your destiny. But he can't have it! (Psalm 138:7)

"I have told you all this so that you may have peace in me. Here on earth, you will have many trials and sorrows. But take heart, because I have overcome the world." (John 16:33)

THE LONG HAUL

TRAVELING TEARS

Have you ever been so hurt that you couldn't even pray? All you could do was weep. (Psalm 6:6)

See, it's okay when all you can do is cry. Because when you do, it shows your need for God and wanting Him to act on your behalf. (Psalm 18:6)

Remember, your tears are prayers too, and they travel to God when you can't speak. (Psalm 39:12)

"To the LORD I cry aloud, and He answers me from His holy mountain. Selah" (Psalm 3:4)

THE LONG HAUL

NO GARBAGE

Folks will always have something to say, but just because they say it, doesn't make it true.

See, your worth isn't determined by what others say about you. So, despite what they think or say, God created you, and He makes no mistakes or garbage. (Numbers 23:19) (Isaiah 45:18)

Remember, don't forget your value because of someone else's ignorance. (Ephesians 4:18)

"For you created my inmost being; you knit me together in my mother's womb. I praise you because I am fearfully and wonderfully made; your works are wonderful; I know that full well." (Psalm 139:13-14)

THE LONG HAUL

AFTER THE TEST

Let's face it; there aren't many people who will happily volunteer to take a test. But in life, you're going to have them and trials.

If you haven't experienced sorrow or hardships yet, keep living because it's coming. But you can also rejoice. (Romans 5:1-5) (Romans 5:3-4)

Remember, after the test, comes a blessing. So, keep the faith. God is at work! (James 1:2-4)

"Blessed is the one who perseveres under trial because, having stood the test, that person will receive the crown of life that the Lord has promised to those who love him." (James 1:12)

THE LONG HAUL

YELLING FROM THE ROOFTOP

Have you ever fought so hard to be heard or to save your name? See, as much as you want to yell from the rooftops to prove you're right, it's not for you to do. (Deuteronomy 3:22)

Remember, you might not want to, but the only thing you need to do is be still and hold your peace. God has you and the situation! (Exodus 14:13-14)

"He will make your righteous reward shine like the dawn, your vindication like the noonday sun. Be still before the LORD and wait patiently for him; do not fret when people succeed in their ways, when they carry out their wicked schemes." (Psalm 37:6-7)

THE LONG HAUL

REPAIRED OR REPLACED

Have you ever been so focused on repairing something that no matter what you did to try to fix it, there was no going back to its original state?

See, there is nothing wrong with trying to fix what's broken. But sometimes, you can't reconstruct what's permanently damaged. (Proverbs 26:11)

Remember, you can't repair what God is replacing. (Isaiah 43:19)

"Behold, the former things have come to pass, and new things I now declare; before they spring forth, I tell you of them." (Isaiah 42:9)

THE LONG HAUL

APOLOGY NOT NECESSARY

An apology is warranted when you do something you want to acknowledge an offense for. But are you apologizing when you shouldn't?

See, if someone from your past keeps bringing up the fact you've changed, and you aren't who you used to be. That's a good thing and doesn't justify a sorry. (Isaiah 43:18-20)

Remember, you owe no one an apology for becoming whom God has called you to be. (1 John 5:4-5)

"Therefore, if anyone is in Christ, he is a new creation. The old has passed away; behold, the new has come." (2 Corinthians 5:17)

THE LONG HAUL

THE RESCUE

Have you ever been in trouble and called out to a friend or a loved one to help, yet no one came?

See, you have to change who you're calling out to. The Lord's word is clear, "Call upon me in the day of trouble. And I will rescue and deliver you." (Psalm 50:15)

Remember, if you need help, you must call on the name of the Lord, and He will save you. (Romans 10:13) (Joel 2:32)

"And it shall be *that* everyone who shall call upon the name of *the* Lord will be saved." (Acts 2:21)

THE LONG HAUL

IT'S SIMPLE

You say you won't, but the doubt, anxiety, and worry still creep in. Sound familiar?

See, when you decide to take the worst scenario possible and worry, you're saying, "I don't trust God." And there is nothing you're going through that He isn't aware of and can't handle. (Jeremiah 32:27) (Luke 1:37)

Remember, it's simple, STOP WORRYING and trust God! (Proverbs 3:5)

"Do not be anxious about anything, but in everything by prayer and supplication with thanksgiving let your requests be made known to God." (Philippians 4:6)

THE LONG HAUL

NEGATIVE OUTCOMES

Your thoughts have power. So, the magic question is: What are you thinking?

See what you think will set the path for your destiny. And if you allow the enemy to continue to run rampant in your head, it will lead to nothing good. (John 10:10)

Remember, negative thinking leads to negative outcomes.

"For as he thinketh in his heart, so *is* he." (Proverbs 23:7)

THE LONG HAUL

IT'S THE LANGUAGE

Some folks speak English, while others speak a variety of other languages. So, the question is: What is yours?

See, your language is what you say to yourself. And if you're constantly speaking belittling words and the opposite of what God says about you, then you should quit talking. (Ephesians 4:29)

Remember, it's time to change your language. (Isaiah 55:11)

"Death and life are in the power of the tongue, and those who love it will eat its fruits." (Proverbs 18:21)

THE LONG HAUL

____

____

____

____

____

____

____

____

____

PEACE IS SACROSANCT

There are thousands of quotes on peace. And ultimately, they all come down to one thing. It's priceless.

See if something or someone in your life is costing you your peace, it's too expensive. Therefore, it's time to let it go. (1 Corinthians 14:33)

Remember, your peace is sacrosanct, so protect it!

"And a harvest of righteousness is sown in peace by those who make peace." (James 3:18)

THE LONG HAUL

A WATCHED POT NEVER BOILS

Let's face it, having to wait on God to act on your behalf can be challenging. But it's better to wait than wish you did. (Proverbs 3:5-6)

See, a watched pot never boils. In other words, you sitting and trying to rush God to act isn't going to make Him do it. (Lamentations 3:25)

Remember, His time, not yours! (Ecclesiastes 8:6)

"Therefore, the Lord waits to be gracious to you, and therefore He exalts himself to show mercy to you. For the Lord is a God of justice; blessed are all those who wait for Him." (Isaiah 30:18)

THE LONG HAUL

JUST LIKE THAT

Life happens just like that. But so does God. (Acts 16:25-34) Don't be surprised at the fiery trials that test you in life. They might shock you, but God already knows about them. (1 Peter 4:12-13) (Isaiah 46:10) (Jeremiah 29:11)

Remember, God specializes in SUDDENLY. So, get ready. (1 Kings 3:13)

"Now to the *One* being able to do exceedingly above all things that we ask or think, according to the power working in us." (Ephesians 3:20)

THE LONG HAUL

TIE THEM UP THIS WAY

Some folks mean well when they try to tell you how they would handle what you're going through. But the truth is, they're not you.

See, you have to be careful taking advice from those who haven't been where you are. In other words, if they've never been to Paris, how can they tell you about an experience there? (Proverbs 14:8)

Remember, if they haven't been in your shoes, they have no business telling you how to lace them. (Proverbs 4:26)

"Only simpletons believe everything they're told! The prudent carefully consider their steps." (Proverbs 14:15)

THE LONG HAUL

FOR HOW LONG

When you hold on to anger and resentment, that's called a grudge. So, the question is, how long will you hold onto it?

See, being mad way after the incident occurs causes the root of bitterness. And when that happens, it can hurt you more than the person who inspired it. (Psalm 37:8)

Remember, let go of the grudge and give yourself the peace you deserve. (John 16:33)

"Get rid of all bitterness, rage and anger, brawling and slander, along with every form of malice." (Ephesians 4:31)

THE LONG HAUL

THE DIET

Let's face it; some folks care a lot about how they look. This means they watch what they eat and work out rigorously to look great. But does the same come into practice for what they watch and hear? (1 Timothy 4:8)

See, your diet and health are not only what you eat and partake in. But it's also what you watch and what you listen to as well. (Luke 21:34)

Remember, be mindful of the things you put into your body: emotionally, spiritually, and physically.

"Do you not know that your bodies are temples of the Holy Spirit, who is in you, whom you have received from God? You are not your own; you were bought at a price. Therefore, honor God with your bodies." (1 Corinthians 6:19-20)

THE LONG HAUL

OPEN VENTS

There's nothing wrong with venting out your grievances every once in a while. However, is the person you're opening up to a trusted source?

See, everyone doesn't mean you well. In other words, they could smile in your face, but secretly wish you harm. (Matthew 7:15)

Remember, venting to folks can be dangerous. Why? Because open vents lead into different rooms, you don't want to be in. (1 John 4:1)

"But false prophets also arose among the people, just as there will be false teachers among you, who will secretly bring in destructive heresies, even denying the Master who bought them, bringing upon themselves swift destruction." (2 Peter 2:1)

THE LONG HAUL

____

____

____

____

____

____

____

BRACES CORRECT THE SMILE

Just as a parent corrects a child, God does the same. (Deuteronomy 8:5)

See, it's easy to be happy-go-lucky when God is in the blessing business in your life, but His business is also in correction. And although you may not like it, it's necessary. (Psalm 94:12)

Remember, braces hurt when they're first applied, but they will correct your smile.

"I correct and discipline everyone I love. So be diligent and turn from your indifference." (Revelation 3:19)

THE LONG HAUL

NOTICE SERVED

When you're tired, you're TIRED. That means that throwing in the towel seems better than pressing through. But it's in those moments that quitting shouldn't be an option. (Philippians 3:14)

See, the enemy will attack your mind, affecting your emotions, causing doubt, and leading you to quit. But that's when you doubt your doubts and feed them with faith. (Matthew 21:21)

Remember, serve notice to the enemy, and tell him to GO! Why? Because you're not giving up or giving in! (2 Corinthians 2:14) (Galatians 6:9)

"But as for you, be strong and do not give up, for your work will be rewarded." (2 Chronicles 15:7)

THE LONG HAUL

____

____

____

____

____

____

____

RIGHT IN THE EYE

It might be hard to believe, but the fact is that all snakes are not legless. Some have two legs that walk around daily, looking you straight in the eye, which you might call "friend." (Matthew 7:15)

See, the serpent is craftier than any other beast. So, if you're not alert and sober-minded, the most poisonous scorpions might be under your nose. (1 Peter 5:8-9)

Remember, dogs will look down when they do something wrong, but snakes will look you right in the eye. BE WISE! (Matthew 10:16)

"I have given you authority to trample on snakes and scorpions and to overcome all the power of the enemy; nothing will harm you." (Luke 10:19)

THE LONG HAUL

____

____

____

____

____

____

____

PUFFED WITH CONCEIT

You know the folks. They have an opinion about everything, and with the words that come from their mouth, it's the gospel. Why? Because they're know-it-alls. (Romans 1:22)

See, only God knows everything. And only a fool thinks they can't be taught. And when you continue to be puffed with conceit, you demonstrate that you actually know nothing. (1 John 3:20) (Proverbs 28:26) (1 Timothy 6:4)

Yes, you're strong. Therefore, be strong enough to bend and be teachable. (Hosea 4:6)

"Woe to those who are wise in their own eyes and clever in their own sight." (Isaiah 5:21)

THE LONG HAUL

IT'S A SIN

When you don't trust God, that's worry. And worry is a sin. See, you can't say you live by faith and trust God. Because if your life is walking by faith, you know God is in control. But when you turn to worry, you're saying the opposite. Therefore, you're declaring that God isn't your Source. (2 Corinthians 5:7) (Romans 14:23)

So, if you're looking for a cure to worry - TRUST GOD!!!! (Proverbs 3:5-6)

"They do not fear bad news; they confidently trust the LORD to care for them." (Psalm 112:7)

THE LONG HAUL

WHAT HE WANTS

Let's face it; folks want what they want when they want it. But that doesn't mean it's what God has planned. (Isaiah 65:2)

See, God's plans for you are not of evil or harm. Therefore, He wants what's best, so your plans won't always be His. (Jeremiah 29:11)

Remember, God knows best. So don't fret if it didn't work out your way. His way is better. (1 Peter 4:2)

"My thoughts are nothing like your thoughts," says the LORD. "And My ways are far beyond anything you could imagine. For just as the heavens are higher than the earth, so My ways are higher than your ways and My thoughts higher than your thoughts." (Isaiah 55:8-9)

THE LONG HAUL

____

____

____

____

____

____

____

SHUT FOR A REASON

No one wants a door slammed in their face. But all doors that close aren't by accident. (Psalm 139:2-3)

Sometimes God has to close what you refuse to walk out of. And if you keep forcing your way back in and staying, don't be surprised if He kicks you back out. (Proverbs 3:5-6)

Remember, you can't keep banging on doors that God wants permanently closed. (Isaiah 22:22)

"What he opens no one can shut, and what he shuts no one can open." (Revelation 3:7)

THE LONG HAUL

THE UNDERSTANDING OF WHY

Life happens, and sometimes, folks will obsess about understanding why.

See, as much as you might want to escape the hardships and trials you will go through. And you will. You can't! Because they help you grow. (James 1:3-6)

Remember, stop replaying it repeatedly in your head and rid yourself of the raging emotions. Peace is more important than driving yourself crazy to comprehend what happened. Let it go, and let God work out His plan! (Ephesians 4:31-32) (Isaiah 43:18-19)

"Trust in the LORD with all your heart, and lean not on your own understanding; in all your ways acknowledge Him, and He will make your paths straight." (Proverbs 3:5-6)

THE LONG HAUL

____

____

____

____

____

____

CREATED BY YOU

It's easy to point the finger when someone else causes you pain. But are you quick to hold yourself accountable when you inflict self-wounds?

See, just as important as it is for others to be held responsible for their actions. You, too, must be liable for the damage you've caused. (Proverbs 9:12)

Remember, you can't keep playing the victim by the circumstances you created. (Galatians 6:5)

"Yes, each of us will give a personal account to God." (Romans 14:12)

THE LONG HAUL

DON'T LEAVE ME

It never feels good when someone you love leaves you. But it's up to you if you decide to open the door or block them from going. (Proverbs 1:7)

See, it might be a knee-jerk reaction to chase what has left you. But you don't know the reason God has allowed them to go. (Romans 8:28)

Remember, even though they left, God could have moved them for your good. (Psalm 121:5-8)

"They went out from us, but they did not belong to us. For if they had belonged to us, they would have remained with us. But their departure made it clear that none of them belonged to us." (1 John 2:19)

THE LONG HAUL

DON'T MAKE IT PERMANENT

"It's too much; things feel hopeless because it appears so dark and turbulent. And now, the only relief that makes sense is to give up." So, the question is, does that describe you? (Psalm 6:6)

See, it's scary when you're in the thrust of a storm. But the rain and thunder only last for a little while. (Matthew 8:24-27)

Remember, the feeling of defeat is temporary. Giving up is what makes it permanent. (Galatians 6:9)

"Do not be slothful in zeal, be fervent in spirit, serve the Lord. Rejoice in hope, be patient in tribulation, be constant in prayer." (Romans 12:11-12)

THE LONG HAUL

TRYING TO FIGURE IT OUT

Are you quick to say you trust God? However, secretly, you're trying to figure it out yourself.

See, you can't say you have faith and trust God if *"figuring it out"* is your backup plan. To trust God is to have faith to rely solely on Him. (Psalm 9:10 & 28:7)

Remember, it's not for you to understand or figure out how. But trust Him in everything. (Proverbs 3:5)

"Delight yourself in the Lord, and He will give you the desires of your heart. Commit your way to the Lord; trust in Him, and He will act. He will bring forth your righteousness as the light, and your justice as the noonday." (Psalm 37:4-6)

THE LONG HAUL

SUBDUE THE EMOTIONS

When there are highly intense emotions, it can lead to rash decisions. So, do you operate on how you feel?

See, when you're a believer, you walk by faith, not sight. So, no matter how it looks or feels. Your feelings don't dictate what you know God says about the matter. (2 Corinthians 5:7) (1 John 3:20)

Remember, your emotions need to subside before you decide. (Proverbs 29:11)

"But don't let the passion of your emotions lead you to sin! Don't let anger control you or be fuel for revenge, not for even a day. Don't give the slanderous accuser, the Devil, an opportunity to manipulate you!" (Ephesians 4:26-27) (TPT)

THE LONG HAUL

REHEARSING THE PAIN

Some people mean good. However, others love to inflict pain. That's why it's imperative to discern whom you allow in your space. (1 John 4:1)

See, no one is exempt from past hurt and pain. Yes, it happened, and you must move on. But if you've let it go, and others haven't, it's time to let them go too. (Romans 8:1)

Remember, remove the people who keep making you rehearse your pain. (2 Corinthians 5:17)

"I—yes, I alone—will blot out your sins for my own sake and will never think of them again." (Isaiah 43:25)

THE LONG HAUL

EASIER SAID THAN DONE

God makes it very clear that you should not be anxious about ANYTHING. That means whatever has you worrying and freaking out - STOP! (Philippians 4:6-8)

See, you might be thinking, *Easier said than done.* But it is as simple as that. And once you give that worry to God, He will work it out. (1 Peter 5:7)

Remember, God never panics, so why are you? (Matthew 6:27-34, 11:28-30)

"Now, may the Lord of peace himself give you peace at all times in every way. The Lord be with you all." (2 Thessalonians 3:16)

THE LONG HAUL

THROWING GREASE ON FIRE

When you're trying to put out a fire, the last thing you should do is throw grease on it. And just like high-burning flames, drama occurs the same. (Proverbs 26:20)

See, you can't go where some folks are going, and you can't be involved with their issues. In other words, their spectacle has nothing to do with you. (James 3:5)

Remember, you can't let other people's drama suffocate you to where God is taking you. (2 Timothy 1:9)

"Be very careful, then, how you live—not as unwise but as wise, making the most of every opportunity, because the days are evil. Therefore, do not be foolish, but understand what the Lord's will is." (Ephesians 5:15-17)

THE LONG HAUL

____

____

____

____

____

____

____

ABCDEFG...

You learn your ABCs by singing the Alphabet Song as a child. And if someone sang it differently, you would know they've placed the letters out of order.

See, your life might not be letters flowing from the famous song. But if your path isn't going as planned, you can't halt because things seem out of sequence. (Isaiah 8:10)

Remember, your life isn't going to be in the order you think. But by God's plan and design. (Psalm 33:10-11) (Jeremiah 29:11)

"You can make many plans, but the LORD's purpose will prevail." (Proverbs 19:21)

THE LONG HAUL

LOOK WHO'S HOLDING THE KNIFE

Being betrayed, whether personally or professionally, hurts to the core. Especially when you didn't see it coming, but what stings the most is when you look back to see who caused you to bleed. (Psalm 41:9)

See, hurt people hurt people. Therefore, don't let your gut reaction be to pierce them back. (1 Samuel 24:12)

Remember, it isn't the stab that causes the pain. It's turning around and seeing who's there holding the knife. (Job 19:19)

"Don't say, 'I will get even for this wrong.' Wait for the LORD to handle the matter." (Proverbs 20:22)

THE LONG HAUL

HUSH YOUR SPEECH

Words are a lot like stones, and folks love to throw them. But not all love to deal with the repercussions of the wound they cause. (Matthew 12:37)

See, there's tremendous power in what comes out of your mouth. And controlling your speech can determine your life. (Proverbs 13:3, 18:21)

Remember, your words are forceful. So, hush your speech if it's causing damage. (Ephesians 4:29)

"For, Whoever would love life and see good days must keep their tongue from evil and their lips from deceitful speech." (1 Peter 3:10)

THE LONG HAUL

____

____

____

____

____

____

____

CHOOSING DISTANCE

You can love folks, but it doesn't mean they should remain in your life.

Sometimes, people can bring heartache, pain, and destruction to your world. And you can love them, but it doesn't mean they should be around you. (Psalm 119:29)

Remember, choosing distance isn't about being mean, but having peace of mind. (Psalm 34:14)

"Let us therefore make every effort to do what leads to peace and to mutual edification." (Romans 14:19)

THE LONG HAUL

A PRISON SENTENCE

It's a beautiful thing to be loyal to someone. But you must be careful not to be devoted to a fault. (Matthew 7:15)

See, the love and devotion for others shouldn't be to your death. And if they don't appreciate what you bring to the table, then it's time for you to get up. (Matthew 10:13-14)

Remember, your loyalty doesn't mean a prison sentence.

"They must turn from evil and do good; they must seek peace and pursue it." (1 Peter 3:11)

THE LONG HAUL

ARE YOU OKAY?

Every day, people are strolling in life. And though they appear to smile and laugh the day away, the truth is you never know what they're going through. (John 16:33)

See, not everyone wants to blurt out their trials and pain. So, painting a picture of rainbows and unicorns is easier than showcasing heartache. (Psalm 143:7-8)

Remember, depression might look like a smile. So, ask these three little words, "Are you okay?" (Proverbs 12:25)

"The Lord GOD has given Me the tongue of discipleship, to sustain the weary with a word. He awakens Me morning by morning; He awakens my ear to listen as a disciple." (Isaiah 50:4)

THE LONG HAUL

A SHEPHERD OR A KING

Folks are always going to have an opinion. And sometimes their viewpoint is on you.

See, your value will never decrease based on someone's inability to see your worth. And when people judge, it speaks volumes about them, not you! (Matthew 7:1-5)

Remember, David's brothers saw a shepherd. However, God saw a King. It's simple; God defines you, not others. (Genesis 37:12-27, 41:37-44)

"Now if we are children, then we are heirs—heirs of God and co-heirs with Christ, if indeed we share in his sufferings in order that we may also share in his glory." (Romans 8:17)

THE LONG HAUL

IT'S ALL MY FAULT

It's all my fault. That's the lie the enemy tries to get you to believe. But he's a liar! (John 8:44)

See, the enemy wants your mind. And if you don't protect it, you'll be a victim of the thoughts he plants. (1 Peter 5:8)

Remember, the battle is lost when you let the enemy's lies weaken your mind. But there's good news: God has given you authority to overcome the enemy's power. Therefore, he has none! So, nothing will harm you. (2 Corinthians 11:3) (2 Timothy 1:7) (Luke 10:19)

"We take captive every thought to make it obedient to Christ." (2 Corinthians 10:5)

THE LONG HAUL

BLEEDING HANDS

It hurts when people want to leave. But do you know what hurts more? Bleeding hands trying to hold on to them. (Romans 8:18)

See, it doesn't matter if it's a job, a relationship, or a person. There is a season and time for everything. And when it's up, you must let it go. (Ecclesiastes 3:1-8)

Remember, if they want to walk out, hold the door open for them. (Isaiah 43:18-19)

"They went out from us, but they did not really belong to us. For if they had belonged to us, they would have remained with us; but their going showed that none of them belonged to us." (1 John 2:19)

THE LONG HAUL

WASTED WORDS

Let's face it; some folks love to talk. But sometimes you can talk too much. (Proverbs 10:19)

See, silence is a source of great strength. (Lao Tzu) And as much as you want to have the last word. Some speech doesn't need utterance. (Proverbs 29:11)

Remember, stop wasting words. The best thing you can say is nothing at all. (Job 13:5)

"Even fools are thought wise if they keep silent, and discerning if they hold their tongues." (Proverbs 17:28)

THE LONG HAUL

IT'S ALL DARK

Has life ever been so dark for you that the only things you see are your trials and hardships right before you? (John 14:27)

See, you have to walk by faith and not sight. So, your trust in God must be bigger than any fears you face. (2 Corinthians 5:7) (John 14:27)

Remember, stop being afraid of what's in front of you because God is with you. (Isaiah 41:10-13) (Psalm 27)

"Even when I walk through the darkest valley, I will not be afraid, for you are close beside me. Your rod and your staff protect and comfort me." (Psalm 23:4)

THE LONG HAUL

WHAT THEY DON'T TALK ABOUT

The truth is, EVERYONE goes through something. And how they deal with it varies.

Contrary to popular belief, hurt and depression don't always look like blackout rooms and crying profusely while lying in bed. Often, it's getting up and heading to work, the grocery store, or church, all with a smile on your face. While inside, your heart is bleeding out. (Psalm 34:17-18)

So, before you talk about or judge anyone, pray for them. You have no idea the silent battles they're facing. (Psalm 102) (James 5:16)

"And God shall wipe away all tears from their eyes; and there shall be no more death, neither sorrow, nor crying, neither shall there be any more pain: for the former things are passed away." (Revelations 21:4)

THE LONG HAUL

____

____

____

____

____

PRUNING OUT THE JUDASES

Who wants to get betrayed? No one! But unfortunately, it happens. (Psalm 41:9)

Yes, it will be a knee-jerk reaction to cry and even scream out of anger from the betrayal. But that's the last thing you should do. Instead, rejoice. Why? Because God will always prune folks out of your life, that means you know good. (Genesis 50:20)

Remember, God sees a Judas before you do. (Psalms 121:7-8) (Proverbs 15:3)

"The Lord is faithful, and He will strengthen and protect you from the evil one." (2 Thessalonians 3:3)

THE LONG HAUL

LIPSTICK ON A PIG

You can put lipstick on a pig, but it's still a pig at the end of the day.

See, the proverbial saying is true, *Everything that glitters isn't gold.* You can't be deceived by what appears to be shiny and glittery. When in reality, it's a fake. (1 Thessalonians 5:22)

Remember, discern the difference between pure gold and gold plated. (1 Samuel 16:7)

"Look beneath the surface so you can judge correctly." (John 7:24)

THE LONG HAUL

____

____

____

____

____

____

____

____

____

LET ME GET THIS OFF MY CHEST

It's no big surprise that some folks aren't going to be happy for you. In other words, misery loves company. (James 3:16)

See, there are no exemptions to problems with anyone. And although a good healthy venting session gets things off your chest, it doesn't mean you should do it. (Ecclesiastes 9:17)

Remember, be careful sharing your woes with someone who's glad you have them. (Ecclesiastes 5:2)

"Set a guard, O LORD, over my mouth; keep watch over the door of my lips!" (Psalm 141:3)

THE LONG HAUL

TRAINING WHEELS

Training wheels are used to help children learn how to ride bicycles. In a nutshell, they're a guide to keep them from falling.

See, you also have a training wheel, and He's called God. So, when you fall or if someone purposely knocks you down, He's right there picking you back up and helping you peddle on. (Proverbs 24:16)

It's easy. Let God help you on your ride. *(life's journey)* (Joshua 1:9)

"Though they stumble, they will never fall, for the LORD holds them by the hand." (Psalm 37:24)

THE LONG HAUL

____

____

____

____

____

____

____

____

RELAX – TRUST GOD

Waiting is the last thing you want to do when you want something. But trying to force it can be at a cost. (2 Peter 3:9)

See, when you decide to force what you want, that causes tension. Which produces stress because you don't have the patience to wait for God. (Job 13:15)

Remember, relax, and trust God to do what He does best. (Hebrews 6:15)

"'Therefore, wait for me,' declares the LORD." (Zephaniah 3:8)

THE LONG HAUL

WHAT YOU HAD

Folks often want what they don't have and forget to give thanks for their blessings.

See, the very thing you could be complaining about right now, someone else would be rejoicing to have it. (1 Thessalonians 5:18)

Remember, start appreciating what you have before it becomes what you had. (James 4:6)

"Giving thanks always and for everything to God the Father in the name of our Lord Jesus Christ." (Ephesians 5:20)

THE LONG HAUL

BE LIKE RUTH

The story of Ruth in the Bible is one of heartbreak and loss, but ends with a divine destiny. (Ruth 1)

See, trials and storms will come into your life. There is no escaping it. But you must decide if you will remain heartbroken or press forward with what God has in store for you. (Philippians 3:13-14) (Jeremiah 29:11)

Remember, take a page from the story of Ruth. She didn't go back to what was familiar. She walked into the unknown, and God blessed her. (Ruth 2,3 4)

In other words, don't be afraid of your next – God is with you! (Joshua 1:9)

"So do not fear, for I am with you; do not be dismayed, for I am your God. I will strengthen you and help you; I will uphold you with my righteous right hand." (Isaiah 41:10)

THE LONG HAUL

____

____

____

____

____

NOT THE SAME

Whether you like it or not. Someone imitating you is a form of flattery. (Proverbs 29:5-6)

See, it will be frustrating seeing anyone duplicate what you've originated. But no matter what someone tries to recreate, you will always be the original. (Thessalonians 1:6)

Remember, let them steal your recipes or style. But guess what? It won't be the same. (Proverbs 20:17)

"Dear brothers and sisters, pattern your lives after mine, and learn from those who follow our example." (Philippians 3:17)

THE LONG HAUL

RUINED WITH AN EXPLANATION

You can say you're sorry. However, as soon as you use the word *"but,"* the apology seems void.

It's simple; apologizing takes humility. And true humility is recognizing God's power and His retribution for condemning if you don't aim toward righteousness. (Micah 6:8) (Proverbs 22:4)

Remember, don't ruin an apology with an explanation.

"Therefore, as God's chosen people, holy and dearly loved, clothe yourselves with compassion, kindness, humility, gentleness and patience." (Colossians 3:12)

THE LONG HAUL

YOU DON'T HAVE TO ANSWER

When your phone rings, it's a knee-jerk reaction to answer. However, you're not obligated to pick up just because someone is calling. (1 John 4:1)

See, the truth is not everyone reaching out to you means you well. And answering the call could lead to your disturbance. (Hebrews 5:14)

Remember, your peace is priceless; you don't have to answer. (Hebrews 4:12)

"And it is my prayer that your love may abound more and more, with knowledge and all discernment, so that you may approve what is excellent. And so, be pure and blameless for the day of Christ." (Philippians 1:9-10)

THE LONG HAUL

____

____

____

____

____

____

____

TRYING TO UNDERSTAND

Have you ever had the phone ring only to receive devastating news? How about an email that's not in your favor? I can give many scenarios, but often they lead to the same question: *Why God?* (Romans 11:33)

John 13:7 says it all: Jesus replied, "You do not realize now what I am doing, but later you will understand."

See, no matter what you're going through, you must rejoice. Because even through difficult circumstances, God is still working for your good. (1 Peter 4:13) (Romans 8:28)

Remember, God has a reason for allowing what happens. It's okay not to understand; just trust His will. (Proverbs 3:5)

"For I consider that the sufferings of this present time are not worth comparing with the glory that is to be revealed to us." (Romans 8:18)

THE LONG HAUL

THE INTERPRETATION OF DIFFICULT

Let's face it; no one wants to go through a difficult time. But the fact is you will. However, the Lord is with you during it all. (Isaiah 41:10)

See, what's hard to you, isn't for God. He declares that all things become possible when you believe Him in your situation. (Mark 9:23)

Remember, don't interpret "difficult" as impossible. (Luke 1:37)

"Ah, Lord God! It is You who have made the heavens and the earth by Your great power and by Your outstretched arm! Nothing is too hard for You." (Jeremiah 32:17)

THE LONG HAUL

YOU'RE WASTING YOUR TIME

If you want to waste your time, resume with worry regarding the problems you have. (1 Peter 5:7)

I get it! You have a lot going on, and you probably think no one understands what you're going through. WRONG!

See, God does, and He also has an expiration date for your storm. (Mark 4:39)

Remember, you will lose your joy and peace of mind if you continue to be concerned about what God is already working out. (John 14:27)

"Let not your hearts be troubled. Believe in God; believe also in me." (John 14:1)

THE LONG HAUL

BEING COMPLACENT

When you're comfortable, it's what you know, and the thought of leaving can be stressful. But necessary. (2 Corinthians 5:17)

See, when you need to grow, the process of change begins. Therefore, where you want to stay complacent, God makes moves. (Ecclesiastes 7:14)

Remember, God cares more about your growth than your comfort. (Joshua 1:9)

"I will lead the blind by ways they have not known, along unfamiliar paths I will guide them; I will turn the darkness into light before them and make the rough places smooth. These are the things I will do; I will not forsake them." (Isaiah 42:16)

THE LONG HAUL

WHEN GOD KILLS IT

Sometimes what you want isn't what God wants for you. And if you don't have the courage to let it go, He will intervene. (Romans 8:34)

See, God knows everything. Therefore, He watches and protects you even when you don't think you need it. (Proverbs 15:3) (Psalms 121:7-8)

Remember, often, God kills things before they kill you. So, TRUST HIM! (Job 13:15)

"Trust in the Lord with all your heart, and do not lean on your own understanding." (Proverbs 3:5)

THE LONG HAUL

TWO TYPES OF TIRED

There are times when you are tired because you haven't gotten enough sleep, leading to exhaustion. Then you have the one where your mind and soul become restless dealing with life trials. So, the question is, which describes you?

See, often, folks are weary because they're trying to handle what they need to turn over to God. And if a person continues to carry what they need to release, they will never find rest. (Psalm 55:22)

Remember, you need rest and peace. So, give it to God. (1 Peter 5:7)

"Come to me, all who labor and are heavy laden, and I will give you rest. Take my yoke upon you, and learn from me, for I am gentle and lowly in heart, and you will find rest for your souls. For my yoke is easy, and my burden is light." (Matthew 11:28-30)

THE LONG HAUL

____

____

____

____

____

____

SHUTTING UP THE ENEMY

One thing is for sure; the enemy loves to try to take you out. And often, he attacks with lies. (John 8:44)

See, you might be at the point where you're ready to fight your adversary. But you have to know how to fight, and it's one not with hands nor revenge. (Deuteronomy 32:35)

Remember, praise will shut the enemy's mouth! (James 5:13)

"From the mouths of children and infants You have ordained praise on account of Your adversaries, to silence the enemy and avenger." (Psalm 8:2)

THE LONG HAUL

THE WAR IN THE MIND

One of the biggest lies many folks believe is the one the enemy plants in their mind. (Philippians 4:8)

See, the mind is powerful. This is why the enemy loves to instigate a war there to steer you away from God onto negative thoughts. (Romans 12:2)

Remember, take capture of your thoughts by focusing them only on God. (2 Corinthians 10:5)

"And the peace of God, which surpasses all understanding, will guard your hearts and your minds in Christ Jesus." (Philippians 4:7)

THE LONG HAUL

WOUNDED BY EVIL

The devil loves to strike. And when he throws darts, they're fiery, piercing to the soul. (Ephesians 6:16)

See, even when you put on the whole armor of God, it's still up to you to determine how you allow the puncture to affect you. (Ephesians 6:11-13)

Remember, when wounded by evil, you can be bitter or better. Which are you? (Ephesians 4:31)

"See to it that no one fails to obtain the grace of God; that no "root of bitterness" springs up and causes trouble, and by it many become defiled." (Hebrews 12:15)

THE LONG HAUL

HE FORGIVES

Once you apologize for a wrong you've committed, you can't make the other person accept the apology. (Proverbs 28:13)

See, regardless of the scale of harm. God still wants you to confess your sins. Why? Because He is faithful and forgives sins and cleanses from all unrighteousness. (1 John 1:9)

Remember, there is nothing God won't forgive.

"In Him we have redemption through His blood, the forgiveness of our trespasses, according to the riches of His grace." (Ephesians 1:7)

THE LONG HAUL

EASY, BREEZY, BEAUTIFUL

When things are like the iconic tagline from Covergirl, *"Easy, Breezy, Beautiful."* There are no worries. But what about when they go bad?

The truth is that even when life is difficult, you still have to trust God. See, God doesn't lie. Therefore, His Word, strength, and reliability are true. (Numbers 23:19) (1 John 5:20) (1 Thessalonians 5:24)

Remember, base your life on God and not your circumstances. (Proverbs 3:5)

"Trust in Him at all times, O people; pour out your hearts before Him. God is our refuge. Selah" (Psalm 62:8)

THE LONG HAUL

____

____

____

____

____

____

____

YOUR RED SEA

Let's face it; everyone struggles with something. And often, running seems like the answer, but what happens when you run into a dead-end? (Hebrews 4:16)

I get it; you feel alone and abandoned. As God has forgotten about you, but just like the Israelites ran into the Red Sea and didn't think they could cross, God was still with them. And He's with you too. (Exodus 14)

Remember, don't panic about the circumstances you're facing. God will remove what is blocking you from moving forward. (Psalm 107:6)

"So, you see, the Lord knows how to rescue godly people from their trials, even while keeping the wicked under punishment until the day of final judgment." (2 Peter 2:9)

THE LONG HAUL

____

____

____

____

____

____

THE CONCERN

The battle you're in is concerning. But don't think for a second God's not aware of it. (Isaiah 46:9–11)

See, the enemy has a way of getting you to focus on your woes instead of God. But the fact is, there is NOTHING that you're going through that God can't handle. (Ephesians 6:11-17) (Jeremiah 32:17)

Remember, don't let your difficulties become louder than the voice of God. (Romans 10:17) (Isaiah 26:3)

"Do not fear [anything], for I am with you; Do not be afraid, for I am your God. I will strengthen you, be assured I will help you; I will certainly take hold of you with My righteous right hand [a hand of justice, of power, of victory, of salvation]." (Isaiah 41:10)

THE LONG HAUL

SETTLING THE SCORE

Seeking vengeance for the wrong that has been done to you might feel sweet, but it doesn't mean you should pursue it. (Romans 12:19)

See, it's the infamous tit-for-tat—the pursuit of retaliation for the hurt you've suffered. But the retribution doesn't belong to you. (Deuteronomy 32:35)

Remember, if you want to settle the score, wait for God to avenge. (Proverbs 20:22)

"May the LORD judge between you and me. And may the LORD avenge the wrongs you have done to me, but my hand will not touch you." (1 Samuel 24:12)

THE LONG HAUL

DIRTY WATER

No matter what you do, there will always be someone who won't like you. (Psalm 38:19)

The truth is, who cares what haters say or do? They still can't halt the blessings of God for your life. (Isaiah 54:17)

Remember, dirty water won't stop a plant from growing. In other words, the negativity the enemy throws at you won't stop your progress. (Psalm 18:17) (Psalm 118: 6-7)

So, keep growing and stay focused on God. (1 Samuel 2:26)

"Everyone will hate you because of me. But not a hair of your head will perish. Stand firm, and you will win life." (Luke 21:17-19)

THE LONG HAUL

THE HARD TRANSITION

One thing is for sure, change and transition can be challenging. But it's necessary. (Ephesians 4:22-24)

See, when you're moving to another level in life. You have to think of it like seasons in the weather. In other words, at some point, it ends, and you adjust to the temperature, whether it's winter, spring, summer, or fall. (Daniel 2:21) (Ecclesiastes 3:1-8)

Remember, no one says this new beginning is going to be easy. But you're not in it alone; this will grow you for the better. (Joshua 1:9) (Ephesians 4:13-16) (Jeremiah 12:2)

"Therefore, if anyone is in Christ, he is a new creation. The old has passed away; behold, the new has come." (2 Corinthians 5:17)

THE LONG HAUL

____

____

____

____

____

____

____

1,000 MPH

When you have many worries, it can feel as if your mind is racing a thousand miles per hour. And all for what? (Philippians 4:6)

Yes, what you're going through is hard, but it's not too hard for God to handle. Therefore, you need to let it go and give it to Him. (Jeremiah 32:17) (1 Peter 5:7)

Remember, rest your mind; God has you! (Isaiah 26:3)

"And the peace of God, which surpasses all comprehension, will guard your hearts and your minds in Christ Jesus." (Philippians 4:7)

THE LONG HAUL

TRIP WITHIN THE FIRST STEP

Let's face it; some folks always have something to say about your choices. But so, what? (Proverbs 18:8)

See, it's easy for people to THINK they know your story. But the truth is they don't have a clue. (James 4:11)

Remember, if everyone who commented on your life walked in your shoes, they would trip in the first step. (Deuteronomy 32:35)

"Obviously, I'm not trying to win the approval of people, but of God. If pleasing people were my goal, I would not be Christ's servant." (Galatians 1:10)

THE LONG HAUL

TROUBLING AFFLICTION

Many folks are going through trials, storms, and hardships. Yet, all are asking the same question. "When will this end?"

See, God does NOTHING to harm you, and there is a purpose for the storm you're in. It's rain that allows plants to grow. Therefore, your harvest is sprouting. (Jeremiah 29:11) (Leviticus 26:4)

Remember, it might be today, tomorrow, or next week. But God has an expiration date for your troubling affliction. (Galatians 6:9) (James 5:7)

"And after you have suffered a little while, the God of all grace, Who has called you to His eternal glory in Christ, will Himself restore, confirm, strengthen, and establish you." (1 Peter 5:10)

THE LONG HAUL

THE PIGGY BANK

Children often had what was known as a piggy bank, growing up. A container that you put coins in for later. But when they needed the money, it was shaken or broken to get it out. (Deuteronomy 28:12)

The truth is that people are a lot like piggy banks. In other words, what's inside you is valuable; and God often has to shake and even break you to get it out. (Matthew 14:19)

See, the heartbreak and brokenness you feel aren't about your circumstances but what God is doing in your life. (Genesis 32:22-32) (Hebrews 12:7)

Remember, it might feel bad, but God is working it out for your good! (Romans 8:28)

"For our present troubles are small and won't last very long. Yet they produce for us a glory that vastly outweighs them and will last forever!" (2 Corinthians 4:17)

THE LONG HAUL

____

____

____

____

____

HOMEWORK

A student of any age typically will receive homework in an area of study. Why? So they can learn. (Proverbs 22:6)

See, there's nothing wrong with helping someone you love. But sometimes, your help can go too far. In other words, they will never learn their lesson if you do their assignment. (Proverbs 13:24) (Proverbs 22:15)

Remember, it's not your responsibility to learn the lesson God has assigned for someone else. (Proverbs 15:32)

"No discipline seems pleasant at the time, but painful. Later on, however, it produces a harvest of righteousness and peace for those who have been trained by it." (Hebrews 12:11)

THE LONG HAUL

THE REBUTTAL

Whether you want to or not, no matter how much you want to give a rebuttal, God needs you to be quiet. (Proverbs 17:28)

See, it might feel good to get the hostility off your chest. But there is obedience in silence. (Ecclesiastes 3:7)

Remember, discern the difference between knowing when to speak and when to be silent. (Hebrews 5:14)

"Understand this, my dear brothers and sisters: You must all be quick to listen, slow to speak, and slow to get angry." (James 1:19)

THE LONG HAUL

WHO'S MAD?

The anger, bitterness, and revenge you want will eat you alive if you won't let it go. (Ephesians 4:31)

See, you have to be okay without an apology. Meaning the person that wronged you—you still must forgive. Even when they don't own up to the pain they've caused you. (2 Corinthians 2:10)

Remember, stop being mad. Seek your peace by letting it go. God will take care of it. (Psalm 4:4) (Romans 12:19)

"But the wisdom from above is first pure, then peaceable, gentle, open to reason, full of mercy and good fruits, impartial and sincere." (James 3:17)

THE LONG HAUL

____

____

____

____

____

____

____

SHOUT! YOU ALREADY WON

No one wants to be in a fight they think they've lost. But thanks be to God, who already gives us the victory through Christ Jesus. (1 Corinthians 15:57)

See, you have to have faith that no matter what you're facing, God already knows about it and has it worked out. (1 John 5:4) (Isaiah 46:9-11)

Remember, God says, *your battle is already won.* So, give Him praise. (Romans 8:37) (James 5:13)

"But I have raised you up for this very purpose, that I might display My power to you, and that My name might be proclaimed in all the earth." (Exodus 9:16)

THE LONG HAUL

____

____

____

____

____

____

____

____

HANGING ON BY A THREAD

A broken heart can make a person feel like life is coming out of their soul. But regardless of the circumstances that caused the pain, God is with you in it. (Joshua 1:9) (Psalm 34:18)

I get it; you think you're in your storm alone, and no one understands what you're going through. But that's not true because God does, and before you had the affliction, He saw it coming and planned a purpose to use it. (Jeremiah 29:11) (Romans 8:28)

Remember, when you're hanging on by a thread, it's God who holds it. (Isaiah 41:10-13, 49:16)

"For He [God] Himself has said, 'I will not in any way fail you nor give you up nor leave you without support. I will not, I will not, I will not in any degree leave you helpless nor forsake nor let [you] down (relax My hold on you)! [Assuredly not!]'" (Hebrews 13:5) (AMPC)

THE LONG HAUL

____

____

____

____

____

____

STRUGGLING TO BREATHE

When a fire starts, it quickly produces a cloud of black smoke and will fill a room with darkness. And if you're there, you'll begin to struggle to breathe because of it. (Hebrews 12:29)

See, you might not be in an actual fire, but one similar that's called a furnace of affliction. And nothing is worse than being in the battle of your life and thinking God has left you there to die. And that's just not true. Because He is always there with you and protects you from the flames. (Isaiah 48:10) (Isaiah 43:2)

Remember, God, won't let you burn, no matter how hot it gets. (Daniel 3:8-25)

"And give relief to you who are troubled, and to us as well. This will happen when the Lord Jesus is revealed from heaven in blazing fire with his powerful angels." (2 Thessalonians 1:7)

THE LONG HAUL

____

____

____

____

____

____

____

YOU'RE DROWNING ME

Let's face it; sometimes, you can care more about someone than they do themselves. And there comes a time that you have to leave them to swim in their sorrow. (Proverbs 26:11)

See, it's not your responsibility to carry others' loads. And if you continue to be their lifeguard, you will find yourself sinking with them. (Galatians 6:5)

Remember, stop drowning trying to save everyone. (Jeremiah 17:10)

"For we must all appear before the judgment seat of Christ, that each one may receive his due for the things done in the body, whether good or bad." (2 Corinthians 5:10)

THE LONG HAUL

BLAME IT ON ME

A story has three sides: Yours, Theirs, and the Truth. And no matter how much you want to vent your woes, you should be silent. (Lamentations 3:26)

See, God sees everything and judges those according to their actions. And even if you are not at fault, it's for God to handle, not you. (Hebrews 4:13) (2 Corinthians 5:10)

Remember, sometimes you must say, *"Blame it on me."* Because at the end of the day, they may have been responsible for your hurt, but you are responsible for the healing. (Psalm 107:20)

"Then let the heavens proclaim his justice, for God himself will be the judge." Selah. (Psalm 50:6)

THE LONG HAUL

GOD SENT

When you're in trials and tribulations, it's hard to see God working, but the fact is He is. (James 1:2)

See, there is nothing you're going through that's being wasted. So, no matter what the enemy tries to plant in your mind. All things are working together for your good. (Ephesians 6:11) (Romans 8:28)

Remember, when fiery trials happen, it's because God sent it or He's going to use it. (1 Peter 1:6, 4:12)

"No discipline seems pleasant at the time, but painful. Later on, however, it produces a harvest of righteousness and peace for those who have been trained by it." (Hebrews 12:11)

THE LONG HAUL

____

____

____

____

____

____

____

____

THE VEIL

Life has a way of hitting hard like a Tsunami. While some folks ride the waves, others fall in and almost drown. (Psalm 107:28-31)

See, despite what you think you may know of someone. The truth is you have no clue what they're dealing with. (Matthew 18:33)

Remember, as believers in Christ, you must be kind to your neighbor. But more importantly, check in on them, for many are fighting for their lives, all while wearing a veil. (John 13:34-35)

"Keep on loving each other as brothers and sisters. Don't forget to show hospitality to strangers, for some who have done this have entertained angels without realizing it!" (Hebrews 13:2)

THE LONG HAUL

REGARDLESS OF WHAT YOU SEE

Do you focus on your problems or God when trouble hits your life? (Colossians 3:2)

See, it might be a knee-jerk reaction to focus on your woes. But when you do that, you take your eyes off God. (Hebrews 12:2)

Remember, God's Word is true, regardless of what it looks like. Therefore, He has YOU and your problems all worked out. (Numbers 23:19) (Isaiah 41:10)

"Look, I am with you, and I will watch over you wherever you go, and I will bring you back to this land. For I will not leave you until I have done what I have promised you." (Genesis 28:15)

THE LONG HAUL

A PRACTICE FIELD

Your heart is valuable and should always be protected. So, the question is, do you guard it? (Philippians 4:6-7)

See, your heart is constantly under attack. And without a covering, it can turn into an unhealthy one. Which can have a devastating impact on your life. (Psalm 73:26)

Remember, your heart isn't a practice field to be played on. Protect it! (Proverbs 23:19)

"Above all else, guard your heart, for everything you do flows from it." (Proverbs 4:23)

THE LONG HAUL

IMPOSSIBLE SITUATIONS

Many believers face what is commonly known as *impossible situations*. And although it can lead to feelings of heartbreak and frustration to endure. You're made for it. (Philippians 4:13) (Ephesians 3:16)

See, it's the enemy's trick to make you THINK there's no way out of what you're going through. But there is a way out, and God is with you in the dark valley. (John 8:44) (Ephesians 6:11-12) (Psalm 23:4)

Remember, you're not weak, but built with the foundation of God to withstand any storm. (Matthew 7:24-25) (Isaiah 28:16)

"And when the flood arose, the stream beat vehemently against that house, and could not shake it, for it was founded on the rock." (Luke 6:48)

THE LONG HAUL

DUST YOURSELF OFF

Have you ever wanted something so badly that no matter what you did, it just didn't work? (Psalm 73:26)

See, failing isn't a bad thing. It's designed to teach you. But importantly, it's what you do after the failure that counts. (2 Timothy 3:16-17)

Remember, it's okay. Now dust yourself off and try again! (Proverbs 24:16) (Romans 3:23-24)

"Arise, shine, for your light has come, and the glory of the LORD rises upon you." (Isaiah 60:1)

THE LONG HAUL

I'M FINISHED WITH YOU

Whether folks get mad or not, boundaries are necessary. (1 Corinthians 15:33)

See, sometimes you have to love people from afar. Now—that doesn't mean you have to be surly. But you're not required to be in their presence either. (1 John 4:1) (Philippians 1:9-10)

Remember, forgive, but also be finished! (Matthew 6:14-15)

"It is for freedom that Christ has set us free. Stand firm, then, and do not let yourselves be burdened again by a yoke of slavery." (Galatians 5:1)

THE LONG HAUL

LET GOD EXPOSE

No matter what conniving and deviating scheme the enemy tries to plot, NOTHING is hidden from the sight of God. (John 10:10) (Ephesians 6:10-18)

See, the weapon can form in your life, but it doesn't mean it will prosper. The fact is God sees EVERYTHING. Therefore, He protects you from all harm. (Isaiah 54:17) (Proverbs 15:3) (Psalm 121:1-8)

Remember, let God expose every trap the enemy plants, and you trust His plan and don't take action. Vengeance belongs to Him. (John 3:20) (2 Chronicles 16:9) (Romans 12:19)

"For the LORD, your God is going with you! He will fight for you against your enemies, and He will give you victory!'" (Deuteronomy 20:4)

THE LONG HAUL

KING, HELPER, & PROVIDER

Many Believers will holler out that they are Christians. While inside, they're full of worry. (Luke 12:25)

See, worry is nothing more than applying the worst-case scenario. Which leads to panic. (Matthew 6:25-34)

Remember, you must get off the treadmill of negative thinking and put your faith and trust in God. He is your King, Helper, and Provider. (Proverbs 3:5) (Hebrews 11:6) (Psalm 54:4)

"You are my portion, Lord; I have promised to obey your words. I have sought your face with all my heart; be gracious to me according to your promise. I have considered my ways and have turned my steps to your statutes." (Psalm 119:57-59)

THE LONG HAUL

NEGATIVE PROJECTED THOUGHTS

Although you're going through some hard times, your mind must be focused on God and not on your struggles. (Colossians 3:2)

See, the enemy wants to destroy you. And once he gets in your mind, he will transform your thoughts into negativity. This is why you must take every thought captive and obey Christ. (John 10:10) (2 Corinthians 10:5)

Remember, stop allowing negative projected thoughts to become your mediation. (Hebrews 4:12) (Romans 12:2)

"And be *continually* renewed in the spirit of your mind [having a fresh, untarnished mental and spiritual attitude], and put on the new self [the regenerated and renewed nature], created in God's image, [godlike] in the righteousness and holiness of the truth [living in a way that expresses to God your gratitude for your salvation]." (Ephesians 4:23-24)

THE LONG HAUL

THE FALSE FRIEND

Listening is essential when communicating. And although it's challenging to remain silent when you want to speak, scripture tells us that too much talk will lead to sin. (Proverbs 10:19)

See, you're practicing self-control when you refrain from talking when you really want to snap and go off. And there is wisdom in taming the tongue. (Proverbs 17:28)

Remember, your tongue can be a false friend. It will cut and do more damage than a knife if not tamed. (Proverbs 12:18)

"Those who guard their mouths and their tongues keep themselves from calamity." (Proverbs 21:23)

THE LONG HAUL

IS IT A DOG OR A WOLF?

When you're younger and innocent as a child, it's easy to trust and open up to anyone. But with age comes wisdom, and your trust becomes sacrosanct. (Job 12:12)

See, not everyone means you well. And it's important to test the spirits you come in contact with to discern if they mean good or evil. (1 John 4:1)

Remember, there is a difference between dogs and wolves. So, be careful whom you trust. (Matthew 7:15)

"Listen! I am sending you out just like sheep to a pack of wolves. You must be as cautious as snakes and as gentle as doves." (Matthew 10:16)

THE LONG HAUL

A BLESSED YES

Who really wants to be told the word NO. Especially when you're earning to hear a YES, but all *"no's"* aren't a bad thing. (Psalm 32:7, 41:2)

See, God always has your best interest in mind. So even when you want something, He knows the harm it will cause. (Psalm 121:7)

Remember, a simple *"no"* is a *"blessed yes"* in disguise. (2 Corinthians 1:20)

"I am with you and will watch over you wherever you go, and I will bring you back to this land. I will not leave you until I have done what I have promised you." (Genesis 28:15)

THE LONG HAUL

DISCONNECT IN PEACE

When you leave people, places, or things, it's not for you to tell the world what happened. (Matthew 7:1-5)

I get it. Wanting to get your side out is a knee-jerk reaction when you've been wronged. But that's not for you to do.

God sees, hears, and knows the truth—No matter how much someone wants to alter it. (Psalm 75:7) (Hebrews 4:13)

Remember, you don't have to defame whom you disconnect from. Just seek peace and move on. (Psalm 101:5) (1 Peter 3:11)

"Turn away from evil and do good; seek peace and pursue it." (Psalm 34:14)

THE LONG HAUL

____

____

____

____

____

____

____

____

FOR YOUR BENEFIT

You're going to wait for all sorts of things in life. And when you get impatient and proceed without God, there's a cost. (Isaiah 40:31) (Lamentations 3:25)

See, God is ALWAYS on time. And just because you're ready for your heart's desire doesn't mean it's aligned with God's plan. (Proverbs 3:5-6) (Jeremiah 29:11)

Remember, every delayed experienced is for your benefit. (2 Peter 3:9) (Jeremiah 29:11)

"Therefore, the Lord waits to be gracious to you, and therefore He exalts himself to show mercy to you. For the Lord is a God of justice; blessed are all those who wait for him." (Isaiah 30:18)

THE LONG HAUL

IS IT PRIDE?

No matter what you've achieved in life or what degree is behind your name, you still don't know everything. (Psalm 139:4) (Proverbs 10:14)

See, pride can be people's downfall. While some folks let their achievements go to their head, they set the precedence of a know-it-all. (Proverbs 16:18) (Matthew 11:27)

Remember, God, is ALL KNOWING. And YOU must be humble, teachable, and willing to learn, regardless of your accolades. (1 John 3:20)

"When pride comes, then comes disgrace, but with humility comes wisdom." (Proverbs 11:2)

THE LONG HAUL

WAITING A LIFETIME

You can sit and wait a lifetime and still not get the apology you deserve. (Isaiah 43:18)

See, when someone hurts you, it's a gratifying feeling when they own their wrong. But you shouldn't sit around waiting for it if they don't either. (Isaiah 65:17)

Remember, it's your job to heal from the pain, even if whoever is responsible never apologizes. (James 5:16) (1 John 4:7-8)

"Be kind to one another, tenderhearted, forgiving one another, as God in Christ forgave you." (Ephesians 4:32)

THE LONG HAUL

NOT WEAK BUT WISE

When you're trying to cultivate joy, it means protecting your peace of mind by any means necessary. (James 4:7-8)

See, you don't have to explain yourself to anyone. And if others don't understand where you're growing and going, that's their problem, not yours. (Psalm 75:7)

Remember, sometimes you must avoid people, places, or things to protect your emotional health. And that isn't a sign of weakness but wisdom. (Philippians 4:6-7) (Isaiah 26:3)

"Be very careful, then, how you live—not as unwise but as wise." (Ephesians 5:15)

THE LONG HAUL

____

____

____

____

____

____

____

____

EATING CROW

Let's face it; there will come a time when you will make a mistake in life. And it's okay because no one is perfect. But the question is: "Can you admit when you're wrong?" (Proverbs 16:18)

I get it! Who wants to be humiliated after taking a stand on a position? But concealing transgressions won't lead you to prosper. (Proverbs 28:13) (Proverbs 22:4)

Remember, you must be willing to eat the crow of correction just as you are eager to devour the congratulations cake. (1 John 1:9)

"If you are wise, you are wise to your own advantage; but if you scoff, you alone will bear the consequences." (Proverbs 9:12)

THE LONG HAUL

THE GRIP

Folks have a way of holding on to people, places, and things that have come to an end. And if they cling too long, their hands begin to bleed. (Isaiah 43:18-19)

When you trust God, it's not about your desires but His will. That means surrendering to His plan and His ways. (Proverbs 3:5-6) (Jeremiah 29:11)

Remember, there's nothing wrong with holding on. Just make sure it's God that you're gripping onto. (Joshua 23:8)

"We must hold on to God's promise that we have said we believed. And we must never let go. He has promised and He will do it." (Hebrews 10:23) (WE)

THE LONG HAUL

____

____

____

____

____

____

____

____

LET ME TEACH YOU A LESSON

Folks often want to be God. In other words, they take what He is supposed to handle among themselves to execute. WRONG! (Romans 13:1-3, 12:17)

See, no matter how much you want vengeance, it doesn't belong to you, but to the Lord. Your job is to leave it alone. (Romans 12:19)

Remember, stop trying to teach someone a lesson God is to teach. (Deuteronomy 32:35)

"Therefore, let the LORD be judge, and judge between you and me, and see and plead my case, and deliver me out of your hand." (1 Samuel 24:15)

THE LONG HAUL

STEER TOWARDS PRAISE

There are a lot of things you could complain about it. But if you do, what have you accomplished? (Psalm 106:25)

I get it! You're going through some trying times. But you should lift your voice in worship instead of murmur in those moments. (1 Corinthians 10:10) (1 Thessalonians 5:18)

Remember, praise prepares your heart for God's Word by steering the attention away from your problems onto His greatness. (Psalm 96:4)

"I will bless the LORD at all times; His praise will always be on my lips." (Psalm 34:1)

THE LONG HAUL

____

____

____

____

____

____

____

____

THE LIFELINE TO JESUS

Everyone will go through something. And when you pray, it's your lifeline to Jesus. (Psalm 34:17-20)

See, God cares for all of us, and because of His unfailing love, we can take all things to Him in prayer. (Psalm 102:17)

Remember, for prayers to be answered, you must first pray. (Philippians 4:6) (Mark 11:24)

"Seek the LORD and His strength; Seek His face continually." (1 Chronicles 16:11)

THE LONG HAUL

____

____

____

____

____

____

____

____

____

EXCEPTIONALLY PHENOMENAL

When your heart has a desire, it's hard to imagine your *(want)* gone. But often, it's for the best. (Philippians 3:13) (1 John 2:19)

See, rejection of any kind is protection. Why? God never takes His best away. So, if it's leaving, there is better in-store. (Isaiah 43:18-19)

Remember, you don't have to beg for anyone or anything. YOU are a gift, the prize, and exceptionally phenomenal. What God is bringing will outshine what has come to an end. (1 Peter 2:4) (Isaiah 43:4, Isaiah 65:17)

"No eye has seen, no ear has heard, no heart has imagined what God has prepared for those who love Him." (1 Corinthians 2:9)

THE LONG HAUL

____

____

____

____

____

____

____

FATHER KNOWS BEST

No one wants to see the plans they've made for themselves fail. But failure is often a blessing in disguise. (Proverbs 1:9)

I get it! You want your way, but your way isn't God's purpose. So, no matter how much you want your plan to proceed, His purpose will always prevail. (Psalm 33:10) (Proverbs 19:21)

Remember, God, your Father knows best, and His purpose will be fulfilled even if your plans aren't. (2 Corinthians 6:18) (Jeremiah 29:11) (Hebrews 6:17)

"The LORD of Hosts has sworn: "'Surely, as I have planned, so will it be; as I have purposed, so will it stand.'" (Isaiah 14:24)

THE LONG HAUL

CALL IT A NIGHT

Sometimes, the thought of giving up seems better than enduring. But there's nothing wrong with thinking about it. The problem lies when you act on those thoughts. (Isaiah 40:29-31)

Blessed is the one who remains steadfast under trial. So even though you may get weary, you'll reap your harvest if you don't give up. (James 1:12) (Galatians 6:9)

Remember, it's better to call it a night than quit! So, rest and get back at it again! (Hebrews 12:11)

"Therefore, my dear brothers and sisters, stand firm. Let nothing move you. Always give yourselves fully to the work of the Lord, because you know that your labor in the Lord is not in vain." (1 Corinthians 15:58)

THE LONG HAUL

____

____

____

____

____

____

STEP ASIDE

If someone was blocking you, you would probably tell them to step aside, right? But what happens when you're the person in the way? (Hebrews 11:6) (Psalm 18:6)

See, when you want God to move on your behalf. You can't be the obstacle blocking Him from doing His work. If so, it's time for you to move. (John 14:13-14) (Isaiah 58:9)

Remember, you called on God to help you. So, step aside. (Psalm 18:6, 91:15)

"I'll gladly step aside and hand things over to you - you can surely save yourself with no help from me!" (Job 40:14)

THE LONG HAUL

I'M NOT OKAY

Often when folks ask someone how they're doing, typically the response is, *"I'm doing great!" "Highly blessed and favored!"* But is that still your response when you're not okay? (Matthew 11:28)

The truth is that you're going to go through multiple seasons in life. Some will bring joy, and others may bring sorrow. But no matter what comes your way, God is with you through it all. (Psalm 46)

Remember, it's okay not to be okay. The Lord is with YOU! (Deuteronomy 31:8-9) (John 16:22)

"Therefore, we do not lose heart. Though outwardly we are wasting away, yet inwardly we are being renewed, day by day. For our light and momentary troubles are achieving for us an eternal glory that far outweighs them all. So, we fix our eyes not on what is seen, but on what is unseen, since what is seen is temporary, but what is unseen is eternal." (2 Corinthians 4:16-18)

THE LONG HAUL

____

____

____

____

A KING/QUEEN BUT A WITCH

Titles merely identify roles. But that doesn't mean you let that be your identity. (Psalm 7:8)

See, it doesn't matter the position you hold. Jezebel was the Queen of Israel and called herself a Prophetess, but she acted like a witch. (1 Kings 16:29-31) (Revelation 2:20)

Remember, you can call yourself whatever you like. But it's your action, character, and integrity that matters. (Proverbs 19:1, 10:9)

"The integrity of the upright guides them, but the crookedness of the treacherous destroys them." (Proverbs 11:3)

THE LONG HAUL

A BLESSING IN DISGUISE

Whether you like them or not, challenges are instrumental in life. And although you may feel they're destroying you, they're actually building you. (James 1:2-4)

See, God never wastes anything that you go through. Every trial, heartbreak, and affliction is working out for your good. (Romans 8:28)

Remember, your calamity is a blessing in disguise. (Acts 13:48)

"And after you have suffered a little while, the God of all grace, who has called you to his eternal glory in Christ, will himself restore, confirm, strengthen, and establish you." (1 Peter 5:10)

THE LONG HAUL

____

____

____

____

____

____

____

____

INCREDIBLE PRESSURE

Everybody wants to be a diamond. But not all can handle the pressure that comes with it. (Proverbs 17:3)

See, God uses the incredible pressure you will face during fiery trials to make you emerge. And yes, your darkest valley and crushing are terrifying. But you'll rise stronger and brighter by them. (Psalm 23:4) (1 Peter 1:7)

Remember, you'll understand the pressure you endured when you truly form into a diamond. (Zechariah 13:9)

"You know that under pressure, your faith-life is forced into the open and shows its true colors. So don't try to get out of anything prematurely. Let it do its work so you become mature and well-developed, not deficient in any way." (James 1:3-4)

THE LONG HAUL

THE HIGH TREE

When God takes you to the next level, expect a bigger devil. Why? Elevation comes with pain. (Jeremiah 29:11)

See, you're like a tree. The higher you are, the more exposure you have to the storm. But it's okay because you're built on the rock. (Matthew 7:24-27)

Remember, God, will take you higher, so expect pain to occur. (Psalm 91:1-16)

"Where they strengthened the believers. They encouraged them to continue in the faith, reminding them that we must suffer many hardships to enter the Kingdom of God." (Acts 14:22) (John 16:33)

THE LONG HAUL

CO-SIGNING MESS

It takes a big person to admit their wrongs, and it doesn't help when you have folks in your circle cheering for your foolery. (1 John 3:7)

See, growth means taking responsibility and ownership of your transgressions. So, no matter what lie you keep telling, God knows the truth, and everyone will give account on judgment day. (Proverbs 28:13) (John 14:6) (Matthew 12:36)

Remember, check your circle. Some of you might be in the company of people co-signing your mess. (Proverbs 13:20)

"Stop being deceived: 'Wicked friends lead to evil ends.' Come back to your senses as you should and stop sinning! For some of you—I say this to your shame—don't fully know God." (1 Corinthians 15:33-34)

THE LONG HAUL

____

____

____

____

____

____

IF I WAS YOU

Sometimes when life hits you with a blow, it's a comfortable feeling to open up to a listening ear. But if they've never been where you are, you shouldn't open your heart to them. (Psalm 141:3)

See, often, folks are quick to tell others what they should and would do if they were them. But the fact is they're not. And if they've never walked in your shoes, they have no business directing your path. (Proverbs 18:21)

Remember, no one has the right to tell anyone to get over something they've never been through. (Proverbs 14:6)

"So let us come boldly to the throne of our gracious God. There we will receive His mercy, and we will find grace to help us when we need it most." (Hebrews 4:16)

THE LONG HAUL

____

____

____

____

____

____

JULY 27

WHEN BIRDS LAND

If someone comes along and pushes you down, that's on them. But if you lay there, that's on you. (Proverbs 24:16)

See, God, has given you authority over the enemy. So, no matter what they try to do, nothing shall hurt you. (Luke 10:19)

Remember, birds are going to fly wherever they want. But you decide if they will build a nest. (1 Peter 1:13)

"In the same way, faith by itself, if it is not accompanied by action, is dead." (James 2:17)

THE LONG HAUL

____

____

____

____

____

____

____

____

____

MY CONDITION

The circumstances that are affecting your life are what is known as a condition. And everyone has one. (Romans 8:18)

See, you're going to be okay. Why? God is your cure. (Psalm 147:3)

Remember, the conditions you're facing aren't your conclusion. (Psalm 23:4) (Revelation 21:4)

"So do not fear, for I am with you; do not be dismayed, for I am your God. I will strengthen you and help you; I will uphold you with my righteous right hand." (Isaiah 41:10)

THE LONG HAUL

____

____

____

____

____

____

____

____

____

____

GOD'S PLAN

There is one thing for sure: *God has a plan for you.* (Jeremiah 29:11)

See, God never said life would be easy. He says, in the world, you will have trouble, but take heart because He has overcome the world. (John 16:33)

Remember, God's plans may not feel good, but they're sure, trustworthy, and faithful. Therefore, in the end, they will be worth it. (Romans 8:18)

"But rejoice insofar as you share Christ's sufferings, that you may also rejoice and be glad when his glory is revealed." (1 Peter 4:13)

THE LONG HAUL

THE GOOD ENGINEER

Controlling folks love to assert power and dominate, especially over their lives. But only one person controls your life—**GOD**. (Psalm 33:10)

See, no matter how much you want your way, God's plan and purpose will always trump what you're trying to regulate. (Proverbs 16:9)

Remember, you have a good engineer, and it's God, so let Him act. (Romans 8:28) (Jeremiah 29:11)

"Many are the plans in a person's heart, but it is the LORD's purpose that prevails." (Proverbs 19:21)

THE LONG HAUL

____

____

____

____

____

____

____

____

HIT WITH A LEFT HOOK

When life throws you a left hook, it's easy to focus on the hit. But when you do that, you take your eyes off God. (Romans 8:5)

See, putting energy into your problems will lead you to act on your emotions. And your feelings are fickle, but God's Word is true. (James 1:22)

Remember, don't focus on what you're seeing and dealing with. Instead, fix your eyes on God. (Hebrews 12:12) (2 Samuel 7:28)

"So we don't look at the troubles we can see now; rather, we fix our gaze on things that cannot be seen. For the things we see now will soon be gone, but the things we cannot see will last forever." (2 Corinthians 4:18)

THE LONG HAUL

LEFT TOO SOON

There is nothing like a good play. And often, when it gets really good, it's time for intermission. (John 8:12)

See, your life is a great play. So yes, there will be trials, heartbreak, pain, and love. But guess what? There's also restoration and healing. (1 Peter 5:10)

Yes—it's scary and dark. But don't make the mistake and leave too soon. (Ecclesiastes 10:4)

Remember, God is just setting up your next scene. So patiently wait and let Him do His good work for you. (Psalm 27:13-14)

"But they who wait for the Lord shall renew their strength; they shall mount up with wings like eagles; they shall run and not be weary; they shall walk and not faint." (Isaiah 40:31)

THE LONG HAUL

____

____

____

____

____

____

STOP TYPING

Nowadays, when folks get mad, they run to their phones, laptops, or iPads to vent their hurt out. But at what cost? (Proverbs 18:24)

See, when you're angry and run to the keyboard, you're giving an audience an open view of your hurt. And some folks love to see you in agony. (Ephesians 4:26–27)

Remember, stop typing and going online. Instead, take what you're going through to the Lord. (Psalm 55:22)

"Give all your worries and cares to God, for He cares about you." (1 Peter 5:7)

THE LONG HAUL

A DEAD END

How many of you have come to the point where life feels like a dead end, and you have no clue what to do? (Proverbs 28:26)

See, it might be easy to sit there and cry at the wall you've encountered. But God needs you to trust Him and have faith. You might not know where to go, but He does. (Psalm 37:23-24) (Proverbs 3:5-6)

Remember, when Moses and the Israelites came to the Red Sea, they thought it was a dead end. But God instructed Moses to put his staff in the water, and it opened up. (Exodus 14:19-31)

In other words, it might look like it's the end. But God always has a plan to see you through. (Jeremiah 29:11)

"The LORD says, 'I will guide you along the best pathway for your life. I will advise you and watch over you.'" (Psalm 32:8)

THE LONG HAUL

____

____

____

____

____

____

YOUR AGENDA

Proverbs 19:21 says that there are many plans in the heart of people, but God's purpose will prevail.

See, no matter how much you're disappointed by your plans being thwarted, God has set you up for His will. And His purpose is better than your agenda. (Proverbs 16:9)

Remember, you have no idea what God has prepared for you. So, stop trying to plan everything and trust Him. (Psalm 33:10)

"Devise your strategy, but it will be thwarted; propose your plan, but it will not stand, for God is with us." (Isaiah 8:10)

THE LONG HAUL

YOU'LL UNDERSTAND LATER

When life happens, folks quickly ask the pivotal question: *Why?* And although there's nothing wrong with wanting an explanation, the truth is God doesn't have to give you one. (Matthew 27:46)

See, you can't be surprised by fiery trials that come to test you. But, on the contrary, you must rejoice—for your difficulties make you partners with Christ. (1 Peter 4:12-13)

Remember, you don't have to drive yourself crazy trying to figure out what God is doing in your life. Instead, trust Him that all things are working for your good. (Romans 8:28)

"Jesus replied, 'You do not realize now what I am doing, but later you will understand.'" (John 13:7)

THE LONG HAUL

DO YOU REALLY HAVE FAITH?

If you say you have faith, but sit and wallow in despair about your circumstances, you don't really have faith, do you? (Matthew 14:31)

See, you will have trials of various kinds, but when you know who you are and whose you are, there's no need to doubt. (John 16:33) (1 John 3:1-2)

Remember, no matter what you're facing; nothing should make you doubt God in your situation. (Isaiah 41:10)

"But when you ask him, be sure that your faith is in God alone. Do not waver, for a person with divided loyalty is as unsettled as a wave of the sea that is blown and tossed by the wind." (James 1:6)

THE LONG HAUL

____

____

____

____

____

____

____

THE DOOR YOU NEVER KNOCKED ON

When you want a door to open, you knock. But what about the ones that you never thought about even approaching? (Revelation 3:20)

See, God has a purpose for you, and His plan will succeed. In other words, He brings you to places you never wanted to go. (Jeremiah 29:11) (Psalm 40:5)

Remember, God is omniscient and sets you up for success. So, expect a door to open that you never thought about knocking on. (Psalm 147:5)

"After this I looked, and there before me was a door standing open in heaven. And the voice I had first heard speaking to me like a trumpet said, 'Come up here, and I will show you what must take place after this.'" (Revelation 4:1)

THE LONG HAUL

____

____

____

____

____

____

DON'T PUT IT BACK ON

Suppose a piece of item you were carrying around weighed you down. Wouldn't you take it off? (Isaiah 9:4)

See, often, folks remove what is holding them back, only to put it back on. But if it weighed you down before, it will weigh you down again. (Isaiah 52:2)

Remember, when God breaks the chains, don't put them back on. (Psalm 107:14)

"In that day, the LORD will end the bondage of his people. He will break the yoke of slavery and lift it from their shoulders." (Isaiah 10:27)

THE LONG HAUL

____

____

____

____

____

____

____

____

A SEASON OF NOT YET

Let's face it; when you want what you want, the last thing you want to hear is—not yet. (Isaiah 40:31)

See, being patient shows you're activating your faith. Simply put, you're telling God, "I trust you." And as soon as you do that, you will survive your season of "Not Yet." (Proverbs 3:5-6)

Remember, patience is your ability to wait for God. (Psalm 27:13-14)

"Therefore, the Lord waits to be gracious to you, and therefore He exalts Himself to show mercy to you. For the Lord is a God of justice; blessed are all those who wait for Him." (Isaiah 30:18)

THE LONG HAUL

HEADS UP

B lows of life can make you bow your head in sorrow. But once you do that, you're right where the enemy wants you. (John 8:44) (2 Timothy 1:7)

See, no matter what you're facing, God says you win. So, there's no need to lower your head with shame or hurt. You have victory. (1 Corinthians 15:57)

Remember, arise, and hold your head up. God has you! (Isaiah 41:10, 60:1)

"The LORD is my light and my salvation; whom shall I fear? The LORD is the stronghold of my life; of whom shall I be afraid?" (Psalm 27:1)

THE LONG HAUL

I NEED TO TALK

Have you ever been talking to someone, and it's apparent they're not listening to you? (Proverbs 2:2)

See, God isn't like humans. Therefore, He can't lie. He says when you cry out to Him, He hears you. But you have to do so first. (Numbers 23:19) (Psalm 34:17)

Remember, if you need someone to talk to, speak to God. He's ready to listen. (Psalm 145:18-19)

"God intended that they would seek Him and perhaps reach out for Him and find Him, though He is not far from each one of us." (Acts 17:27)

THE LONG HAUL

____

____

____

____

____

____

____

____

LEFT OUT

If someone you loved left you out of something essential, and you knew you could help them. How would that make you feel? (1 John 3:1)

See, God loves you so much that He wants to be involved in everything you do. And you can't make a life decision and not include Him. (Jeremiah 31:3)

Remember, stop leaving God out of your life. Keep Him involved. (Ephesians 1:3-10)

"Then Christ will make his home in your hearts as you trust in Him. Your roots will grow down into God's love and keep you strong. And may you have the power to understand, as all God's people should understand how wide, how long, how high, and how deep His love is. May you experience the love of Christ, though it is too great to understand fully. Then you will be made complete with all the fullness of life and power that comes from God." (Ephesians 3:17-19)

THE LONG HAUL

THE TRACK STAR

When problems, trials, and hardships occur. It's often a knee-jerk reaction to run away from them. But that's the last thing you should do. (1 Peter 1:6)

See, there is no better teacher than God Himself. And He teaches through trials. So, your hardships aren't meant to destroy you, but to mold you into the likeness of Jesus Christ. (1 Peter 4:12-13)

Remember, if you want to be a track star, run on a track field in competition, but never away from God and what He's teaching you. (Exodus 4:15) (Psalm 32:8)

"For God called you to do good, even if it means suffering, just as Christ suffered for you. He is your example, and you must follow in his steps." (1 Peter 2:21)

THE LONG HAUL

____

____

____

____

____

____

____

____

I SAW THAT

L et's face it; when someone hurts you deliberately, you want them to pay. But vengeance doesn't belong to you. (Romans 12:19)

See, as much as you want retaliation for your bleeding wound, you can't seek it. God knows and will handle it in His way and in His time. (Deuteronomy 32:35) (Ecclesiastes 3:1)

Remember, don't think God didn't see what they did to you. He did, and He will also take care of it. (Proverbs 15:3)

"Nothing in all creation is hidden from God's sight. Everything is uncovered and laid bare before the eyes of Him to whom we must give account." (Hebrews 4:13)

THE LONG HAUL

RIGHTFULLY DESERVE

How many of you are waiting for someone to say those magical words: I'm Sorry? (Luke 23:34)

I get it! They did you wrong, and you rightfully deserve an apology. But as much as you want it, you must accept that it will probably never happen. And that's okay. (Colossians 3:13)

Remember, even if they never apologize, forgive them anyways! (Luke 17:3-4) (Hebrews 10:30)

"I will take revenge; I will pay them back. In due time their feet will slip. Their day of disaster will arrive, and their destiny will overtake them." (Deuteronomy 32:35)

THE LONG HAUL

____

____

____

____

____

____

____

____

I DON'T WANT TO HOLD YOUR HAND

Jeremiah 29:11 is a popular scripture. And folks are quick to recite it, but do they live it?

See, God does have a plan for your life. But if things don't go your way, that doesn't mean you walk away from Him. Instead, you trust and run to Him. (Proverbs 3:5-6) (2 Peter 3:9)

Remember, you can't say you want God's plan but don't want to hold His hand. (Isaiah 41:10)

"Behold, I have engraved you on the palms of my hands; your walls are continually before me." (Isaiah 49:16)

THE LONG HAUL

THE LAST TIME

No one wants to endure struggles and hardships, but unfortunately, you will. So, the question is: *How do you handle trials when they come?* (James 1:12)

See if you're worried and concerned about your current circumstances, you've forgotten about the last time you were in this predicament. (John 16:33)

Remember, the same God that rescued you before is the same God with you now. (Isaiah 41:10-13)

"And after you have suffered for a little while, the God of all grace, who has called you to His eternal glory in Christ, will Himself restore you, secure you, strengthen you, and establish you." (1 Peter 5:10)

THE LONG HAUL

____

____

____

____

____

____

____

ATTACK OR THOUGHT

Folks are quick to blame satan for causing their attacks. But, often, it's them! (Romans 12:2)

Yes, the enemy does come to destroy. But when you think negative thoughts constantly, that can damage you too. (2 Corinthians 10:3-6)

Remember, maybe you're not under attack, but your thoughts. (Philippians 4:7-8)

"You will keep in perfect peace all who trust in you, all whose thoughts are fixed on you!" (Isaiah 26:3)

THE LONG HAUL

LEFT WITH QUESTIONS

Let's face it; as much as you want closure when something ends, you have to face the fact that you might not get it. But guess what? It's okay! (Isaiah 43:18-19)

See, it's easy to understand when you know the "what" and why of your ending. But unfortunately, when hurt and disrespect are involved—you'll be left with questions. (Proverbs 3:5) (1 John 2:19)

Remember, the disrespect you encountered is your closure. Now move on! (Philippians 3:13)

"Think over what I say, for the Lord will give you understanding in everything." (2 Timothy 2:7)

THE LONG HAUL

____

____

____

____

____

____

____

A LIMITLESS GOD

How many of you are praying for God to do the impossible? Now, how many of you believe He will? (Matthew 19:26)

Ephesians 3:20 says, "Now to him who can do far more abundantly than all that we ask or think." Therefore, God will do the unimaginable—but you must believe. (Luke 1:37)

Remember, God is a limitless God, and He can revive or handle anything you're going through. So, stop putting limits on Him! (Matthew 19:26)

"Great is our Lord, and abundant in power; his understanding is beyond measure." (Psalm 147:5)

THE LONG HAUL

THE SAFETY NET

Would you take a jump if you knew a net would catch you if you fell? (Hebrews 11:6)

See, trusting God means surrendering to Him completely. Therefore, you won't be shaken when contemplating a leap of faith. Why? Because you know whose hands you will fall into. (Proverbs 3:5-6) (Psalms 9:10)

Remember, you have a safety net—it's God. (Psalm 32:7, 37:4-6)

"The one who lives in the shelter of the Most High, who rests in the shadow of the Almighty, will say to the Lord, 'You are my refuge, my fortress, and my God in whom I trust!'" (Psalm 91:1-2)

THE LONG HAUL

____

____

____

____

____

____

____

____

THE CUT-OFF GAME

The reality of life is—everybody doesn't need access to you. (1 Corinthians 15:33)

See, there's nothing wrong with protecting your peace. You should. Therefore, those that try to ruin it shouldn't be around you. (Philippians 4:7)

Remember, it's okay to have a "cut-off game"—cutting people off whom mean you no good. (Proverbs 9:6) (Colossians 3:15)

"Peace I leave with you; my peace I give you. I do not give to you as the world gives. Do not let your hearts be troubled and do not be afraid." (John 14:27)

THE LONG HAUL

GUESS WHO?

Wanting what you want versus God's plan can be challenging. But there's one of you who knows best. Can you guess who? (Proverbs 16:9)

See, there's nothing wrong with wanting your heart's desires. But what you're yearning for might not be the best thing for you. (Psalm 37:4, 145:19)

Remember, it's okay to want what you want. But be careful pursuing what's not God's will. (Romans 12:2) (Proverbs 19:21)

"Now honor the LORD, the God of your ancestors, and do His will." (Ezra 10:11)

THE LONG HAUL

WHO'S LEADING?

Folks are quick to make permanent decisions on temporary emotions. But acting on how you feel will cost you. (Proverbs 29:11)

See, you must be slow in becoming angry. For that type of rage doesn't produce the righteousness of God. (James 1:19-20)

Remember, be led by the spirit of God, not the anger you're temporarily feeling. (Romans 8:14) (Galatians 5:16-24)

"Do not be quickly provoked in your spirit, for anger resides in the lap of fools." (Ecclesiastes 7:9)

THE LONG HAUL

A RED SEA SITUATION

Who wants to deal with a stressful situation? No one. But, unfortunately, you will. (James 1:12)

See, God isn't trying to stress you. And as much as your situation hurts and is probably inconvenient, it isn't meant to destroy you. (Romans 5:3-10)

Remember, God uses *Red Seas Situations* to remind you HE IS GOD! And there is nothing you're facing--He won't see you through. (Exodus 14)

"And after you have suffered a little while, the God of all grace, who has called you to his eternal glory in Christ, will himself restore, confirm, strengthen, and establish you." (1 Peter 5:10)

THE LONG HAUL

WHO'S HAUNTING WHO?

When someone hurts you, it's on them. But how long you allow the heartache to affect you is on you. (Psalm 22:1, 107:20)

See, wounds sting. And often, some injuries bleed more than others, especially if you keep picking at it. (Psalm 147:3)

So, how long will you allow someone else's actions to haunt you? (Ephesians 4:31-32)

"For if you forgive other people when they sin against you, your heavenly Father will also forgive you. But if you do not forgive others their sins, your Father will not forgive your sins." (Matthew 6:14-15)

THE LONG HAUL

____

____

____

____

____

____

____

TAKING FOR GRANTED

Suppose someone didn't appreciate what you've done for them. Would you continue to give them what they're taking for granted? (Proverbs 28:26)

See, some folks are just selfish. And you'll get hurt every time if you continue to expect YOU from them. (Romans 2:8)

Remember, folks don't change by giving them more of what they don't appreciate. (2 Timothy 3:2)

"Behold, I am sending you out as sheep in the midst of wolves, so be wise as serpents and innocent as doves." (Matthew 10:16)

THE LONG HAUL

IT'S FOR YOUR GOOD

Heartbreak, pain, and loss don't feel good. But you can hurt more if you hold on to it. (James 1:2-8)

See, crying and screaming are okay if you're having a bad day. But you have to make sure you don't stay there. In other words, let it bleed, let it hurt. But put a band-aid on it and press on. (Romans 12:12) (2 Corinthians 5:17)

Remember, the uncontrollable and the uncomfortable don't feel good. But it's for your good! (Hebrews 10:36) (James 1:12)

"And we know that God works all things together for the good of those who love Him, who are called according to His purpose." (Romans 8:28)

THE LONG HAUL

IS IT A STORM?

Change can feel extremely uncomfortable. Like a rocky sailboat ride, and some folks can't take it—so they jump ship without giving God a chance to calm the seas. (Mark 4:39)

See, things might be hard. But you have to walk by faith and not by sight. This means— no matter what it looks like, you know God is the captain steering. (2 Corinthians 5:7) (Psalm 89:9)

Remember, it might feel like a storm, but it's exactly your transition into a new season. So, embrace it! (Isaiah 43:19) (Ecclesiastes 3:1-8)

"He changes times and seasons; He removes kings and sets up kings; He gives wisdom to the wise and knowledge to those who have understanding." (Daniel 2:21)

THE LONG HAUL

BEHIND YOUR BACK

Let's face it; enemies can come in disguise as fake friends (Proverbs 27:6)

See, discernment is vital. Because some folks you think are your friends—might be wolves in sheep's clothing. And as soon as trials strike, they're the first to talk behind your back. (Hebrews 5:14) (Matthew 7:15)

Remember, reevaluate those that surround you. You need people praying behind your back and not talking behind it. (Proverbs 13:20) (Psalm 41:9)

"Even my close friend in whom I trusted, who ate my bread, has lifted his heel against me." (Psalm 41:9)

"Therefore, confess your sins to one another and pray for one another, that you may be healed. The prayer of a righteous person has great power as it is working." (James 5:16)

THE LONG HAUL

LET THAT MESS GO

Hostile thoughts aren't good for the soul. But many folks right now are angry. The question is, does that describe you? (Proverbs 14:29)

See, negative feelings stem from the root of bitterness. And when that happens, you'll take your hostility out on everyone. (Hebrews 12:15)

Remember, you have to stop being bitter—just let that mess go! (Psalm 37:8)

"Get rid of all bitterness, rage, anger, harsh words, and slander, as well as all types of evil behavior." (Ephesians 4:31)

THE LONG HAUL

____

____

____

____

____

____

____

____

DON'T PULL ME IN

The best thing you can often do— is mind your own business. (1 Thessalonians 4:11-12)

I'm not saying you shouldn't care about others. But there's a difference between caring and taking on their woes. (Philippians 2:4) (Ephesians 4:32)

Remember, don't let people pull you in their storms when you can barely hold up your umbrella. (Galatians 5:15)

"Better is a handful of quietness than two hands full of toil and a striving after wind." (Ecclesiastes 4:6)

THE LONG HAUL

PURPOSELY TO MISUNDERSTAND

Often, arguments occur because of bad communication. And when someone is adamant about hearing what they want, it doesn't matter what you say. (2 Timothy 2:23-24)

See, some folks are always right—so they think. And you'll drive yourself crazy to get them to comprehend your point. (Proverbs 29:22)

Remember, stop wasting time explaining yourself to people who WANT to misunderstand you. (Titus 3:9)

"And if anyone will not receive you or listen to your words, shake off the dust from your feet when you leave that house or town." (Matthew 10:14)

THE LONG HAUL

____

____

____

____

____

____

____

GREEN LIGHT

R ed lights are warning signals. And as much as you want to ignore them, they're still red. (Romans 1:18-32)

See, God is always speaking, and often He speaks with the answer of NO. So you might keep trying to run down the street, but He will stop you from going around the corner. (John 10:27-28) (Proverbs 16:9)

Remember, those red lights you keep encountering will never turn green, no matter how much you want them to change. (Proverbs 9:9-10, 1:24-33)

"For your obedience is known to all, so that I rejoice over you, but I want you to be wise as to what is good and innocent as to what is evil." (Romans 16:19)

THE LONG HAUL

MY DEADLINE

Folks set deadlines when they're trying to finish something. But what happens when your timeline doesn't meet up with God's? (Proverbs 19:21)

See, you can schedule a day and time for anything you want. But if God isn't ready to give it to you—you'll miss the day every time. (Proverbs 16:9)

Remember, God's timing is better than your deadline. (Ephesians 1:10)

"But do not overlook this one fact, beloved, that with the Lord one day is as a thousand years, and a thousand years as one day." (2 Peter 3:8)

THE LONG HAUL

IS PATIENCE ABSENT?

Let's face it; if you're frustrated, it's because something has occurred that's out of your control. Sound familiar? (Isaiah 41:10)

See, there's nothing wrong with wanting to handle your problem. But what you can do is nothing compared to what God WILL do. (John 16:33) (Romans 8:18)

Remember, your frustration is proof that patience is absent. (Romans 8:25)

"Rejoice in hope, be patient in tribulation, be constant in prayer." (Romans 12:12)

THE LONG HAUL

YET

Some storms feel like they will never end. Yet, they do. (Job 13:15)

See, your situation may be bad. And you could be thinking it's destroying you. Yet, you're still standing. (1 Peter 4:12-13)

Remember, God is a God of YET. Therefore, He will act. (2 Timothy 2:13) (Psalm 71:4)

"Yet I will rejoice in the LORD; I will take joy in the God of my salvation." (Habakkuk 3:18)

THE LONG HAUL

____

____

____

____

____

____

____

____

____

____

HANDLED WITH GRACE

Some people are going to do and say things to you that could be hurtful. But it's up to you to decide on how you will respond. (Leviticus 19:18)

See, folks often react to being hurt with anger and attitude. But what does that solve? (Romans 12:17-21)

Remember, stop reacting out of your feelings. Instead, handle the situation with grace. (James 1:19) (Ephesians 4:29)

"Let your speech always be gracious, seasoned with salt, so that you may know how you ought to answer each person." (Colossians 4:6)

THE LONG HAUL

LEAVE IT CLOSED

Doors open and close all the time. And just because you sit banging on it doesn't mean it will open. (Proverbs 1:7)

You can want entry somewhere, but God knows what's behind it. So, if you trust Him, you can't keep trying to open what He purposely has closed. (Psalm 31:14)

Remember, leave closed doors alone. (Proverbs 15:3)

"Seek the Kingdom of God above all else, and He will give you everything you need." (Luke 12:31)

THE LONG HAUL

THE REPORTER

Nowadays, you have to be careful about people you call friends. Because the truth is, everyone isn't. (1 John 4:1)

See, without discernment, you'll be entertaining a foe that is happy you're going through hell. (Hebrews 5:14)

Remember, some folks are like reporters. They can't wait to report your woes to the world. (Proverbs 20:19)

"Now I urge you, brothers and sisters, keep your eye on those who cause dissensions and hindrances contrary to the teaching which you learned, and turn away from them." (Romans 16:17)

THE LONG HAUL

THE ROBBER

The enemy comes to steal, kill, and destroy. That's a fact. But what about the things you take? (John 10:10)

See, to move on; you have to leave the past behind. And God can't give you what He has in store if you can't release what was. (Isaiah 43:18-19)

Remember, let go of the past. If you keep living there, you'll rob yourself of the future. (Isaiah 65:17)

"But, as it is written, "What no eye has seen, nor ear heard, nor the heart of man imagined, what God has prepared for those who love Him."

THE LONG HAUL

____

____

____

____

____

____

____

____

IT DOESN'T MAKE SENSE

Sometimes life doesn't make sense. And if you try to figure it out, you'll still be wondering. (1 Corinthians 2:13)

See, you might be frustrated going through the most challenging time of your life. But guess what? It's okay. Because it's not for you to understand. (Proverbs 3:5-7)

Remember, when nothing makes sense. That's your cue to trust God. He knows what He's doing, and His plan is greater. (Psalm 37:3-5)

"I am teaching you today—yes, you— so you will trust in the LORD." (Proverbs 22:19)

THE LONG HAUL

THE WORST STORM

Storms come. That's a fact. But they also come to an end. (Psalm 107:29)

See, it might be hard for you to trust God while the winds are tossing the boat in the sea. But just as Jesus was with the disciples on their boat, He's also with you. (Mark 4:35-41)

Remember, Jesus' presence didn't stop the storm, but He helped them through. In other words, you're not in this alone; God is with you. (Deuteronomy 31:6)

"Look, I am with you, and I will watch over you wherever you go, and I will bring you back to this land. For I will not leave you until I have done what I have promised you." (Genesis 28:15)

THE LONG HAUL

____

____

____

____

____

____

____

DELETE IT

O ften, the enemy you're facing is the one in your head telling you lies. (John 8:44) (1 Peter 1:13)

See, if you're saying and thinking anything opposite God's Word and promises for your life, it's a lie. (Ephesians 4:23) (2 Samuel 7:28)

Remember, if the voice you keep replaying isn't of God— delete it now! (Romans 12:2)

"Then they will come to their senses and escape from the devil's trap. For they have been held captive by him to do whatever he wants." (2 Timothy 2:26)

THE LONG HAUL

____

____

____

____

____

____

____

____

HOW'S IT WORKING OUT FOR YOU?

Some folks want to do things their way. The question is, does that describe you? (Jeremiah 18:12)

See, you can continue to be stubborn and do it your way. But God's promises for your life will always prevail. (Proverbs 19:21)

Remember, if you're frustrated and things seem out of control, you're not trusting and giving your cares to God. So, stop! (1 Peter 5:7)

"Because when such a person hears the words of this oath, he invokes a blessing on himself, saying, 'I will have peace, even though I walk in the stubbornness of my own heart.' This will bring disaster on the watered land as well as the dry." (Deuteronomy 29:19)

THE LONG HAUL

____

____

____

____

____

____

____

ROCKING ALL DAY LONG

Worry does no good; it only robs you of the day. So, if you know that, why do you continue to do it? (Philippians 4:6-7)

I get it; you're going through a hard time and don't know how God will fix it. But the fact is, He will. Just like He did it the last time you needed Him. (Hebrews 13:6)

Remember, quit rocking in the chair all day long. God's got you! (Psalm 54:4)

"Fear not, for I am with you; be not dismayed, for I am your God. I will strengthen you, I will help you, I will uphold you with my righteous right hand." (Isaiah 41:10)

THE LONG HAUL

I DON'T LIKE THE ANSWER

Whether you want to believe it or not—unanswered prayers are your answers. (Psalm 32:7)

See, God protects you even when you think you're not in harm's way. So, you might want it, but He knows what's best. (Psalm 41:2)

Remember, if you're frustrated by God not answering your prayers. He did—you might just not like the answer. (Proverbs 3:5-6)

"The LORD keeps you from all harm and watches over your life." (Psalm 121:7)

THE LONG HAUL

____

____

____

____

____

____

____

____

IT'S TIME TO PRAY

Are you going through the most challenging time in your life right now? (Psalm 34:17)

I get it; things are hard, and praying is probably difficult. But it's in those times that you have to. (Ephesians 6:18)

Remember, if you're experiencing the hardest time in your life. That is when you must pray the hardest. (Jeremiah 29:12)

"One day Jesus told his disciples a story to show that they should always pray and never give up." (Luke 18:1)

THE LONG HAUL

THE REVEAL

There are some surly folks in this world. And unfortunately, you might have to deal with them sometimes. (Matthew 7:15)

See, you can't control how people are. So even when their words and actions hurt you, your response is what matters. (James 1:19)

Remember, what people do reveals who they are, but how you respond reveals who you are. (Luke 6:27-28)

"But love your enemies, do good to them, and lend to them without expecting to get anything back. Then your reward will be great, and you will be children of the Most High, because he is kind to the ungrateful and wicked." (Luke 6:35)

THE LONG HAUL

DISRESPECTFUL WITH A SHOUT

Often, people say things they don't mean, which is why you should be slow to speak and slow to become angry. (James 1:19)

See, the same respect you demand in life must be the same as you give others. No matter what they do. (Romans 12:10)

Remember, if you're going to be disrespectful with a shout, make sure you don't whisper your apology. (1 Peter 2:17)

"And you yourself must be an example to them by doing good work of every kind. Let everything you do reflect the integrity and seriousness of your teaching." (Titus 2:7)

THE LONG HAUL

WILL YOU BE THERE FOR ME?

No matter how isolated you feel. You're not alone. (Joshua 1:9) See, folks will let you down. So, there's no need to get upset when they do. However, God will always be there—and it's in His arms where you will find comfort and refuge. (Psalm 46:1-11, 62:8)

Remember, what you need is founded in God. Turn to Him! (Psalm 9:10) (Proverbs 3:5-6)

"The LORD will guide you always; he will satisfy your needs in a sun-scorched land and will strengthen your frame. You will be like a well-watered garden, like a spring whose waters never fail." (Isaiah 58:11)

THE LONG HAUL

SWEET REVENGE

How many of you have been hurt? Now, how many of you want to pay back the hurt that was caused? (Leviticus 19:18)

I get it. You want justice. And sweet revenge might make you feel good, but vengeance doesn't belong to you. (Romans 12:19)

Remember, the best revenge is NONE! (Deuteronomy 32:35)

"Do not say, 'I will repay evil;' wait for the LORD, and He will deliver you." (Proverbs 20:22)

THE LONG HAUL

THE BODYGUARD

Bodyguards are skilled security professionals that protect individuals or groups of people. But have you ever thought about your personal guard? (Isaiah 54:17)

See, God knows everything. And He's on duty 24/7. So even if you don't think you're in harm's way, His protection for you is intact. (Psalms 121:7-8)

Remember, you have the best bodyguard—GOD! (2 Thessalonians 3:3)

"You are my hiding place; you will protect me from trouble and surround me with songs of deliverance." (Psalm 32:7)

THE LONG HAUL

____

____

____

____

____

____

____

THE SPOILED BRAT

Do you know any spoiled brats? And before you answer, are you one? (Matthew 18:3)

See, kids aren't the only ones that are bratty and capable of throwing tantrums. Grown adults (Christians) do too. And often, it's when the YES they want from God becomes a NO. (Jeremiah 4:22)

Remember, it's time to grow up—so stop getting mad at the NOs in life. God knows what He's doing. (1 Corinthians 13:11, 14:20)

"But grow in the grace and knowledge of our Lord and Savior Jesus Christ. To Him be the glory, both now and to the day of eternity. Amen." (2 Peter 3:18)

THE LONG HAUL

I WANT TO EAT THE FRUIT NOW

Farmers and gardeners know that when you plant your crop and seed, it doesn't sprout immediately. It takes water, sun, and time. (Genesis 8:22)

See, you're a precious planted seed by God. And although you want your harvest now. You must go through rain, time, and the Son (GOD). (Galatians 6:9) (Deuteronomy 14:2)

Remember, you don't get to eat the fruit the day you plant your seed. So be patient and trust God's process. (2 Corinthians 9:10)

"Dear brothers and sisters, be patient as you wait for the Lord's return. Consider the farmers who patiently wait for the rains in the fall and in the spring. They eagerly look for the valuable harvest to ripen." (James 5:7)

THE LONG HAUL

DO YOU WANT THE PAIN TOO?

Envy is a dangerous, destructive emotion. And if you are carrying it, you need to get rid of it immediately. (James 3:15-16) (1 Peter 2:1)

See, jealousy makes you desire what others have or who they are. But you're looking at them now, and you have no clue the hell they went through to get to whom you see today. (Proverbs 14:30, 23:17)

Remember, be careful of wanting someone else's glory because you must take their pain too. (Proverbs 23:17-18)

"Pay careful attention to your own work, for then you will get the satisfaction of a job well done, and you won't need to compare yourself to anyone else." (Galatians 6:4)

THE LONG HAUL

DEPOSITING FOOLISHNESS

In this world, using discernment is critical for your life. (Hebrews 5:14)

See, everyone doesn't have good intentions for you. This is why you have to guard your heart and mind and be watchful of those you let in. (Proverbs 4:23) (1 Peter 5:8)

Remember, some folks will try to deposit foolishness into your life. When it happens—close the account. (1 John 4:1)

"Be on your guard against false prophets who come to you in sheep's clothing but inwardly are ravaging wolves." (Matthew 7:15)

THE LONG HAUL

____

____

____

____

____

____

____

WHO'S SURPRISED?

L et's face it; as much as some people like surprises, all aren't good. (James 1:2-4)

See, life has a way of throwing the unexpected at you. And although you may be shocked by what's happening, God already saw it coming. (Romans 5:3-5)

Remember, there are no trials that catch God off guard. He's not worried, so neither should you. It is well! (1 Peter 1:6-7)

"Dear friends, do not be surprised at the fiery ordeal that has come on you to test you, as though something strange was happening to you. But rejoice inasmuch as you participate in the sufferings of Christ, so that you may be overjoyed when his glory is revealed." (1 Peter 4:12-13)

THE LONG HAUL

TROUBLED WOES

It's easy to look at someone and judge what they're going through. But they're not the only ones that have gone through something. (Luke 6:37)

See, before you comment on others' trials and sorrows. Did you forget about your troubled woes? (Matthew 7:1-5)

Remember, EVERYONE has a story. So don't keep bringing up someone else's and acting like you don't have a past too. (James 4:11-12)

"So, when you, a mere human being, pass judgment on them and yet do the same things, do you think you will escape God's judgment?" (Romans 2:3)

THE LONG HAUL

____

____

____

____

____

____

____

____

THE BENEFACTOR

Let's face it; some folks want you to have heartache. Especially those who cause it. (Jeremiah 3:23)

See, no matter what someone does to hurt you. The responsibility of healing lies with you. (Jeremiah 17:14)

Remember, healing will always scare those who benefit from your brokenness. Heal anyways! (Psalm 147:3)

"Behold, I will bring to it health and healing, and I will heal them and reveal to them abundance of prosperity and security." (Jeremiah 33:6)

THE LONG HAUL

WALK AWAY

Your destiny will never be tied to those that leave you. And once you understand this, you will never return to the door again. (2 Corinthians 5:17)

See, folks are going to close doors on you. And that's okay. But never stand begging them to reopen it. (Philippians 3:13-14)

Remember, the same door you're banging on; God sees what lies behind it. So, TRUST HIM—and walk away. (Proverbs 3:5-6)

"And if any place will not receive you and they will not listen to you, when you leave, shake off the dust that is on your feet as a testimony against them." (Mark 6:11)

THE LONG HAUL

IT CROSSED MY MIND

You can think whatever you want. But just because you think it, doesn't mean you need to say it. (Romans 12:2)

Yes, keeping your temper in check can be challenging, especially when someone is trying to provoke you. But your response is vital for growth. (James 1:19)

Remember, things might cross your mind, but they don't have to travel to your mouth. (Proverbs 17:28)

"Set a guard, O Lord, over my mouth; keep watch over the door of my lips!" (Psalm 141:3)

THE LONG HAUL

TAKE THE L

Winning seems better than losing. But some losses are wins. (1 Corinthians 15:57)

See, there are prizes with losses and goodbyes. And just because you can't see it yet, it's a blessing in disguise after you lose people, places, and battles. (James 1:12)

Remember, the "L" isn't always easy to take, but God is giving you a win! (Romans 8:37)

"But thanks be to God, who in Christ always leads us in triumphal procession, and through us spreads the fragrance of the knowledge of Him everywhere." (2 Corinthians 2:14)

THE LONG HAUL

THE CUP OF SUFFERING

Everyone suffers—you have, you are, or you will. There's no escaping it. (John 16:33)

See, no one wants to endure hardships. But God is with you through it, and to go and grow deeper in Christ, you will share in His sufferings. (Acts 14:22)

Remember, the cup of suffering is for your good, your growth, and God's glory! (Acts 9:16)

"And if we are children, then we are heirs: heirs of God and co-heirs with Christ—if indeed we suffer with Him, so that we may also be glorified with Him." (Romans 8:17)

THE LONG HAUL

____

____

____

____

____

____

____

YOU HAVE TO WAIT

When you want your problem handled, waiting on God to act will seem like forever. (Psalm 27:14)

See, no matter how much you try to handle your situation; it's not yours to fix. It's God's. (2 Chronicles 20:15)

Remember, God will work this out for you. But you must be patient and wait. (Isaiah 40:28-31)

"And in that day, it will be said, "Surely this is our God; we have waited for Him, and He has saved us. This is the LORD for whom we have waited. Let us rejoice and be glad in His salvation." (Isaiah 25:9)

THE LONG HAUL

____

____

____

____

____

____

____

____

COMFORTED BY LIES

L et's face it; some folks can't handle the truth. The question is, are you one of them? (Proverbs 6:16-19)

See, as much as the truth hurts; it's necessary for healing and growth. And it will set you free. (Galatians 5:1)

Remember, the truth will be uncomfortable to those who are comforted by lies. Don't let that be you. (Psalm 101:7)

"Then you will know the truth, and the truth will set you free." (John 8:32)

THE LONG HAUL

HE DOESN'T NEED HELP

When you pray and ask God to help you do you trust Him to do it? (Psalm 37:5)

See, when you're burdened, you've exhausted your limits to handle the situation. And that's when you should go to God. And He isn't a man that shall lie. So, when He says He will act and take care of it, He will. (Matthew 11:28-30) (Numbers 23:19)

Remember, God doesn't need your help. If you give it over to Him, leave it alone for Him to take care of, not you. (Psalm 55:22)

"Casting all your cares [all your anxieties, all your worries, and all your concerns, once and for all] on Him, for He cares about you [with deepest affection, and watches over you very carefully]." (1 Peter 5:7)

THE LONG HAUL

____

____

____

____

____

____

____

ROTTEN FRUIT FALLS

You will reap what you sow trying to do folks as they did you. (Job 4:8)

See, God is not to be mocked. What you plant sprouts back up. Furthermore, when you're sowing deceitful and wicked schemes on the one that hurt you, it comes at a cost. (Galatians 6:7-8) (Proverbs 22:8)

Remember, stop trying to seek revenge. Whatever rotten fruit is in your life, it will eventually fall by itself. (Deuteronomy 32:35)

"Now go, lead the people to the place I described. Behold, My angel shall go before you. But on the day I settle accounts, I will punish them for their sin." (Exodus 32:34)

THE LONG HAUL

WHY ARE YOU HOLDING THEIR HAND?

If you're not utilizing discernment, you'll hold any hand that reaches out to you. (1 John 4:1)

The truth is you can't control the wolves walking around in sheep's clothing. But you can be sober-minded and alert to those surrounding you. (Matthew 7:15) (1 Peter 5:8-9)

Remember, if someone you're connected to is holding hands with the devil—why are you holding their hand? (1 Corinthians 10:12)

"See to it that no one takes you captive through philosophy and empty deception, which are based on human tradition and the spiritual forces of the world rather than on Christ." (Colossians 2:8)

THE LONG HAUL

____

____

____

____

____

____

____

____

THE GIRAFFE & THE ANT

Some folks are not on your level, and once you realize that, you'll cease arguing with them. (Proverbs 26:4)

You will never see giraffes and ants holding conversations. Why? Because one is tall and the other is small. (Proverbs 9:6)

It's simple—Stop entertaining people not on your level. (1 Corinthians 15:33)

"If you bite and devour each other, watch out or you will be destroyed by each other." (Galatians 5:15)

THE LONG HAUL

____

____

____

____

____

____

____

____

____

____

I CAN'T STAND

It can be hard to stand when you're constantly getting knocked down. But staying down can't be your solution. (Psalm 34:19)

See, God is sovereign. And even when things seem out of control and life throws you down, God is there to catch you. (Isaiah 25:8-9, 41:10-13)

Remember, if you're finding it hard to stand, kneel. God is there with you. (Philippians 4:6)

"Though they stumble, they will never fall, for the LORD holds them by the hand." (Psalm 37:24)

THE LONG HAUL

PROMOTED

When God has a blessing on your life, no devil in hell can stop it from coming to pass. (Genesis 12:2)

See, no matter the fiery darts and schemes the enemy does to make you doubt yourself. God IS STILL going to bless you, even when people think you don't deserve it. (Ephesians 6:16-17)

Remember, not your supervisor or enemy can stop God's promotion for you. (Deuteronomy 28:7-8)

"For not from the east or from the west and not from the wilderness comes lifting up, but it is God who executes judgment, putting down one and lifting up another." (Psalm 75:6-7)

THE LONG HAUL

TRUST YOU OR ME?

Saying you trust God is easy when life is sunshine and rainbows. But do you keep that same stance when thunderstorms come in? (Psalm 9:10, 112:7)

See, when you're faced with a crisis, it might be your knee-jerk reaction to trust your abilities over God's. But what you can do is NOTHING compared to what He will do to fix the situation. (Ephesians 3:19-20)

Remember, God is asking you today: *Are you going to trust you or me?* (Psalm 13:5, 18:2)

"The Lord is my strength and my shield; in Him my heart trusts, and I am helped; my heart exults, and with my song I give thanks to Him." (Psalm 28:7)

THE LONG HAUL

CLINGING TO THE OLD

When you can't let go of what was, you'll have the same recurring dream and be stuck in the past. (Philippians 3:13-14)

See, God never takes your best away. So when it ends, He will replace it with better. But how can He if you keep holding on to what He needs you to let go of? (Deuteronomy 28:8)

Remember, God can't do something new if you want to cling to the old. (Isaiah 43:18-19)

"Therefore, if anyone is in Christ, the new creation has come: The old has gone, the new is here!" (2 Corinthians 5:17)

THE LONG HAUL

____

____

____

____

____

____

____

THE OUTCOME IS HIS

God looks out for you even when you don't have enough sense to know you need His protection. (Psalm 121:7-8)

See, your job is to put your hope, trust, and faith in God. And when He acts, you must believe His plan is always to prosper and not harm you. (Psalm 9:10, 33:20-22) (Jeremiah 29:11)

Remember, when trusting God is to rely on His outcome too. (Psalm 9:10) (Romans 8:28)

"The counsel of the LORD stands forever, The plans of His heart to all generations." (Psalm 33:11)

THE LONG HAUL

THE FAVOR YOU DIDN'T ASK FOR

It's one thing to ask for a favor because you need it. But have you ever thought about the ones you get that you never asked for? (Psalm 121:7-8)

See, people tend to focus only on what's in front of them. While God is viewing from all angles. So, what you think is rejection is God's protection. (Psalm 32:7)

Remember, never cry about being left, dropped, or eliminated by anyone—They did you a favor. (2 Thessalonians 3:3)

"My God, my rock, in whom I take refuge, my shield, and the horn of my salvation, my stronghold and my refuge, my savior; you save me from violence. I call upon the Lord, who is worthy to be praised, and I am saved from my enemies." (2 Samuel 22:3-4)

THE LONG HAUL

THE BLESSING FROM PERSECUTION

People are who they are. And you can't stop them from lying, gossiping, or stabbing you in the back. (Luke 6:22)

See, you will be persecuted when you desire to live a godly life in Christ Jesus. But just because the enemy forms a weapon at you—doesn't mean it will prosper. (2 Timothy 3:12) (Isaiah 54:17)

Remember, the persecution you're experiencing is a blessing in disguise. (1 Peter 3:14)

"Blessed are those who are persecuted for righteousness' sake, for theirs is the kingdom of heaven. "Blessed are you when others revile you and persecute you and utter all kinds of evil against you falsely on my account. Rejoice and be glad, for your reward is great in heaven, for so they persecuted the prophets who were before you." (Matthew 5:10-12)

THE LONG HAUL

SEEKING SANCTITUDE

Protecting your peace is a constant assignment. But you should continue to seek it by all means necessary. (2 Thessalonians 3:16)

See, you should never apologize for wanting sanctitude. And if someone doesn't understand it, that's not your problem. (Psalm 34:14)

Remember, protecting your peace and energy may require you to deny access to people. But guess what? It's okay. (1 Peter 3:11)

"Let us therefore make every effort to do what leads to peace and to mutual edification." (Romans 14:19)

THE LONG HAUL

____

____

____

____

____

____

____

____

A CONFIDENT PLAN

Have you ever had a plan gone awry and had no idea what to do next? (Jeremiah 10:23)

See, you can make all the plans that you want. But ultimately, it's God's design for your life that will come to pass. (Proverbs 19:21)

Remember, be so confident in God's plans that you don't get upset when yours don't work out. (Jeremiah 29:11) (Proverbs 3:5-6)

"Keep steady my steps according to your promise, and let no iniquity get dominion over me." (Psalm 119:133)

THE LONG HAUL

____

____

____

____

____

____

____

____

____

THE RUNNING MOUTH

Gossiping folks get more exercise than anyone. Why? Because they're constantly running their mouths. (Leviticus 19:16) (Proverbs 6:14)

See, no matter what someone says or thinks about you. It's not for you to respond. God sees, hears, and handles your foes accordingly. (James 4:11)

Remember, God will shut the mouths of everyone who speaks against you. (2 Thessalonians 1:6) (Ezekiel 25:17)

"The LORD is known for his justice. The wicked are trapped by their own deeds. Quiet Interlude." (Psalm 9:16)

THE LONG HAUL

____

____

____

____

____

____

____

____

OUT OF BUSINESS

Have you ever been disappointed in your favorite place going out of business? (John 14:1-3)

See, God is never out of business. He's always open and ready for you to bring your worries and cares to Him. (1 Peter 5:7)

Remember, to get what you need from God, you must walk in the door. In other words, GO TO HIM! (Psalm 55:22)

"I will be your God throughout your lifetime—until your hair is white with age. I made you, and I will care for you. I will carry you along and save you. 'To whom will you compare me? Who is my equal?'" (Isaiah 46:4-5)

THE LONG HAUL

____

____

____

____

____

____

____

____

IT'S THEIR STORY

"*You did it.*" "*It's your fault.*" "*You're the problem.*" Those phrases will always be said when someone doesn't want to take accountability and blame you. (Romans 14:12)

See, you have to be okay with being the villain. *Why?* Because it's their story. And at the end of the day—God knows the truth. (John 8:32, 14:6)

Remember, it's God that vindicates. You don't have to issue press releases to get your side out. Let it go! (Isaiah 50:8)

"For God will bring every deed into judgment, with every secret thing, whether good or evil." (Ecclesiastes 12:14)

THE LONG HAUL

____

____

____

____

____

____

____

THE ESCORT

Have you ever gotten caught in a storm and had trouble seeing your way through it, but you still made it to your destination? (Matthew 8:23-27)

See, God is with you in the darkest times and the heaviest storms of life. So even when you don't know how to get through, He escorts you. (Leviticus 26:12)

Remember, don't put your focus on the natural trials you're experiencing. But turn your eyes to God. (Colossians 3:2) (Isaiah 41:10)

"You shall walk in all the way that the LORD your God has commanded you, that you may live, and that it may go well with you, and that you may live long in the land that you shall possess." (Deuteronomy 5:33)

THE LONG HAUL

____

____

____

____

____

____

THE INTERNAL BLEEDER

Someone is walking around right now, desperately wanting to heal. But they can't quit picking at the wound long enough to cure it. Sound familiar? (Psalm 147:3)

See, all lacerations aren't visible. Some bleed internally without ever getting the proper healing. (Isaiah 53:5)

Remember, the best medicine that you can give yourself is Jesus. Faith in Him is your cure. (Jeremiah 17:14)

"Behold, I will bring to it health and healing, and I will heal them and reveal to them abundance of prosperity and security." (Jeremiah 33:6)

THE LONG HAUL

I'M SORRY

Have you ever sought healing that required you to forgive someone that wasn't even sorry? (Matthew 6:14-15)

See, folks often focus on the pain caused to them. That they never acknowledge the hurt they did to themselves. (Luke 17:3-4)

Remember, you forgave them—now forgive yourself. (Isaiah 43:25)

"In Him we have redemption through his blood, the forgiveness of our trespasses, according to the riches of his grace." (Ephesians 1:7)

THE LONG HAUL

____

____

____

____

____

____

____

____

IT'S CALLED FAITH

Trusting and being faithful to God is easy when you know what's ahead of you. But do you operate the same when facing the unknown? (2 Corinthians 4:18)

See, the same confidence you put in when you see God's plan—needs to be the same assurance when you don't know what's in store. It's called Faith. (Hebrews 11:1)

Remember, nothing ahead of you is bigger than the power of God behind you. (2 Corinthians 5:7) (Deuteronomy 31:8)

"For in this hope we were saved. But hope that is seen is no hope at all. Who hopes for what they already have?" (Romans 8:24)

THE LONG HAUL

BUT IS IT GOD?

Everything that glitters isn't gold. And every opportunity that knocks isn't meant for you to open the door. (Matthew 7:15)

See, discernment is key in life. And without it, you won't be able to distinguish good from evil. (1 John 4:1)

Remember, just because it's presented to you doesn't mean it's from God. (Romans 16:17-18) (Hebrews 5:14)

"And it is my prayer that your love may abound more and more, with knowledge and all discernment, so that you may approve what is excellent; and so be pure and blameless for the day of Christ." (Philippians 1:9-10)

THE LONG HAUL

HOW DO I GET THROUGH?

Have you ever come to a crossroads and didn't know how you would get through? (Joshua 1:9)

When Moses and the Israelites came to the Red Sea, they didn't know what to do either. But God instructed Moses to put his staff in the water and the sea was parted. (Exodus 14:16)

See, you might feel stuck and have no idea what to do, but you're not in the storm alone. (Exodus 13:21)

Remember, God is your helper. Seek Him for your way out. (Psalm 28:7)

"So, we say with confidence: "The Lord is my helper; I will not be afraid." (Hebrews 13:6)

THE LONG HAUL

SOME CAN'T COUNT

Have you ever counted on someone, and then they let you down? (Psalm 18:3)

See, some folks you counted on can't count. And that's okay because your destiny isn't tied to those who leave you. (1 John 2:19)

Remember, stop focusing on who let you down. It's God who lifts you up. (Psalm 40:2)

"I will exalt you, LORD, for you lifted me out of the depths and did not let my enemies gloat over me." (Psalm 30:1)

THE LONG HAUL

____

____

____

____

____

____

____

____

NO THANKS, I'LL KEEP MY OWN

Suppose you threw everybody's problem up in the air that you know. And once they land, would you want to pick up someone else's woes or keep your own? (1 Thessalonians 5:16-18)

See, as hard as things might be for you, it could be worse. And the fact that you are still standing proves that God has you covered. (Psalm 106:1, 121:7-8)

Remember, there is always something to be thankful for. (Colossians 3:15-17)

"Therefore, as you received Christ Jesus the Lord, so walk in Him, rooted and built up in Him and established in the faith, just as you were taught, abounding in thanksgiving." (Colossians 2:6-7)

THE LONG HAUL

WATCH THEM EARS

Everybody isn't for you. And once you realize that, you can discern between good and evil. (Hebrews 5:14)

See, the enemy comes to steal, kill, and destroy. And often, he will use a *"friend"* in disguise to contaminate your ears. (John 10:10) (1 John 4:1)

Remember, be mindful of the voice you listen to. (1 Peter 5:8)

"Make the heart of this people dull, and their ears heavy, and blind their eyes; lest they see with their eyes, and hear with their ears, and understand with their hearts, and turn and be healed." (Isaiah 6:10)

THE LONG HAUL

____

____

____

____

____

____

____

GIVE UP OR GET UP?

It's easy to sit and wallow in your despair, but just because you can do it doesn't mean you should. (Psalm 126:5)

See, God isn't attracted to your problems but to your praise. So instead of complaining, thank Him in advance for everything working out for your good. (1 Thessalonians 5:18)

Remember, do you really want to give up or get up and press on with Christ? (Philippians 3:14) (Romans 8:18)

"So, let's not get tired of doing what is good. At just the right time we will reap a harvest of blessings, if we don't give up." (Galatians 6:9)

THE LONG HAUL

HOW LONG DO I HAVE TO READ THIS PAGE?

Do you feel like you're in the worst chapter of your life? (James 1:2-4)

See, life is like a book. Some pages are fantastic, while others are filled with trials and sorrows. But you can't close the book if you want to see how the story ends. (1 Peter 5:10)

Remember, this is only one chapter; you must keep turning the page to see what God has in store for you. (Isaiah 64:4)

"Now all glory to God, who is able, through his mighty power at work within us, to accomplish infinitely more than we might ask or think." (Ephesians 3:20)

THE LONG HAUL

____

____

____

____

____

____

____

I ACCEPT YOUR APOLOGY

Forgiving someone that has hurt you gives you peace. But it doesn't mean you have to restore the relationship. (Ephesians 4:32)

See, you can't control when or if someone will hurt you. However, you can control whether you will continue dealing with them. (Mark 11:25)

Remember, forgiveness doesn't mean welcoming them back into your life. (James 5:16)

"Remove me from the path of deceit and graciously grant me Your law." (Psalm 119:29)

THE LONG HAUL

POINTING THE FINGER

When someone else is at fault, it's easy to direct any anger you have at them. But what about when you're the culprit? (Proverbs 21:2)

See, everything isn't the enemy. Sometimes the hell you find yourself in is due to your actions. (2 Corinthians 5:10)

Remember, before you point your finger, make sure you're not the weapon that formed against yourself. (Matthew 7:3-5)

"Whoever conceals his transgressions will not prosper, but he who confesses and forsakes them will obtain mercy." (Proverbs 28:13)

THE LONG HAUL

____

____

____

____

____

____

____

____

CONSUMING THE FORMER & FORWARD

If you want to move forward, you can't continue to consume the former things simultaneously. One has to go. (Philippians 3:12-14)

See, it will be challenging to let go of what you know. But you must release the old to get what God has in store. (Ephesians 3:20)

Remember, it's time to discharge the former and embrace the new. (Isaiah 43:18-19)

"Therefore, if anyone is in Christ, he is a new creation. The old has passed away; behold, the new has come." (2 Corinthians 5:17)

THE LONG HAUL

LISTENING SECOND

Are you quick to shout out what you think before you listen? (James 1:19)

See, you must guard your mouth. Why? Because everything you're thinking doesn't need to be said. (Proverbs 13:3)

Remember, only fools speak first and listen second. (Proverbs 18:7)

"The wise store up knowledge, but the mouth of the fool invites destruction." (Proverbs 10:14)

THE LONG HAUL

____

____

____

____

____

____

____

____

____

THERE'S NOTHING BEHIND THE DOOR

Have you ever gotten upset because a door you wanted to go through was closed in your face? (Ephesians 4:26-27)

See, it's disappointing to have a desire right in your grasp. But suddenly, it's taken. (Proverbs 3:5-6)

Remember, God never takes His best away. So don't continue to cry over a closed door with nothing behind it. (Romans 8:28)

"I know all the things you do, and I have opened a door for you that no one can close. You have little strength, yet you obeyed my word and did not deny me." (Revelation 3:8)

THE LONG HAUL

PLANTED TO BLOOM

There's a difference when you have to plant a seed and bury another. (Psalm 85:12)

See, you may be in trying times and don't see the light at the end of the tunnel. But you can't focus on how dark it is but on what God has promised. (Isaiah 26:3)

Remember, God hasn't buried you; He's planted you to bloom. (Ezekiel 36:30)

"Then I will give you rain in due season, and the land shall yield her increase, and the trees of the field shall yield their fruit." (Leviticus 26:4)

THE LONG HAUL

THE BLOCK

The enemy loves to see you rattled and shaken up. But he has no power. (Luke 10:19)

See, no matter what your foe tries to do to you, God says, YOU WIN! So, they can give their best shot, but no weapon formed against you shall prosper. (Deuteronomy 20:4) (Isaiah 54:17)

Remember, NO ONE can block the blessings that God has for you. (Isaiah 14:27)

"Even from eternity I am He, and none can deliver out of My hand. When I act, who can reverse it?" (Isaiah 43:13)

THE LONG HAUL

THE NET

It's easy to say you have faith. But if you're scared to leap—do you really? (Matthew 21:22)

See, believing God is to have faith. It's saying that even though you can't see it, you have the assurance that God has your back and is working it out. (Hebrews 11:1-6)

Remember, it's time for you to jump. Why? Because He has a net ready to catch you. (1 John 5:4)

"What do you mean, 'If I can'?" Jesus asked. "Anything is possible if a person believes." (Mark 9:23)

THE LONG HAUL

BEHIND THE SCENE

It's easy to look at someone and think they have it made. But the truth is you're only seeing the outside. (Matthew 7:15)

See, some folks show you want they want. So, what appears shiny and bright might be rotten to the core. (2 Peter 2:1)

Remember, stop admiring the outer because you don't know what's behind the scenes. (Matthew 23:28)

"Be careful that no one takes you captive through philosophy and empty deceit based on human tradition, based on the elemental forces of the world, and not based on Christ." (Colossians 2:8)

THE LONG HAUL

____

____

____

____

____

____

____

____

THE LIAR

It's simple when someone lies to you, they're a liar. (John 8:44) See, God isn't a man that He shall lie. When He says, He promises to act, He does it. (Numbers 23:19)

Remember, you're putting your trust and focus on the liar when it should be on the One that never lies. (Psalm 89:35)

"This truth gives them confidence that they have eternal life, which God—who does not lie—promised them before the world began." (Titus 1:2)

THE LONG HAUL

THE APOLOGY THAT ISN'T COMING

There's nothing wrong with wanting an apology you rightfully deserve. But how long are you willing to wait for one? (Ephesians 4:32)

See, not everyone can own their mistakes. That's why you have to be okay with a sorry you will never get. (Mark 11:25)

Remember, some folks can't even repent to God, so you know they will never apologize to you! (Luke 13:3)

"The Lord is not slow to fulfill His promise as some count slowness; but He is patient toward you, not wishing that any should perish, but that all should reach repentance." (2 Peter 3:9)

THE LONG HAUL

WHY WAIT?

As much as you want what you want now, life is about waiting. (Romans 12:12)

See, you have to understand that God wants the best for you. And what seems uncomfortable is the process of God's blessing and plan for your life. (Titus 2:13) (Jeremiah 29:11)

Remember, your waiting season isn't punishment; it's preparation. (Isaiah 30:18)

"Wait for the Lord; be strong and let your heart take courage; wait for the Lord!" (Psalm 27:14)

THE LONG HAUL

THE NEVER-ENDING ARGUMENT

Have you ever gone back and forth with someone about who's right or wrong? (Proverbs 29:22)

See, it doesn't mean you're in the wrong when you're in a heated dispute and decide to apologize. (Titus 3:9)

Remember, sometimes you have to say: *I'm Sorry. You're right!* Because valuing your peace is better than the never-ending argument. (Romans 14:19)

"If possible, so far as it depends on you, be at peace with all people." (Romans 12:18)

THE LONG HAUL

IT'S YOUR TURN

Do you offer people grace that need it? But when it comes to yourself, do you have that same leeway? (Colossians 3:13)

See, the same forgiveness you give to others also applies to you. (Mark 11:25)

Remember, you've forgiven everybody else; now it's your turn. (1 John 1:9)

"Then I acknowledged my sin to You and did not hide my iniquity. I said, 'I will confess my transgressions to the LORD', and You forgave the guilt of my sin. Selah." (Psalm 32:5)

THE LONG HAUL

THE YAMMER

There's nothing wrong with voicing your concerns. The problem lies when you can't stop complaining about them. (1 Corinthians 10:10)

See, God isn't attracted to your yammering but to your praise. And there's something to be thankful for in all circumstances. (1 Thessalonians 5:18)

Remember, as much as you pout about it; you should pray about it! (Philippians 4:6)

"Likewise, the Spirit helps us in our weakness. For we do not know what to pray for as we ought, but the Spirit himself intercedes for us with groanings too deep for words." (Romans 8:26)

THE LONG HAUL

____

____

____

____

____

____

____

THE REPLACEMENT

It's hard to let go of what you know. But you will never know what God has for you if you cling to the old. (Isaiah 65:17)

See, God never takes your best away. But to get what He has in store; you must release the old. (Isaiah 43:18-19)

Remember, God will send you a replacement. But it will come when you're not afraid to lose what He's replacing. (Deuteronomy 7:18)

"Instead of your shame you will receive a double portion, and instead of disgrace you will rejoice in your inheritance. And so, you will inherit a double portion in your land, and everlasting joy will be yours." (Isaiah 61:7)

THE LONG HAUL

____

____

____

____

____

____

____

____

THAT 'NO' SAVED YOUR LIFE

A yes always feels good. But what about the *no's* in life? (James 5:12)

God knows everything, so even when you think you are being punished, God protects you from harm. (Psalm 121:7-8)

Remember that a 'NO' from God saved your life. (2 Thessalonians 3:3)

"The Lord will rescue me from every evil deed and bring me safely into his heavenly kingdom. To Him be the glory, forever and ever. Amen." (2 Timothy 4:18)

THE LONG HAUL

CONFIDENT AS A BIRD

It's easy to say you trust God, but if you panic when the storm comes, then your action shows you aren't confident that God is indeed your shelter. (Psalm 46:1)

See, a bird that sits on a tree branch isn't afraid of the limb breaking. Why? Because their trust is in their wings. So even if the branch does break, the bird knows to fly away. (Psalm 9:10) (Matthew 6:26) (Isaiah 40:31)

Remember, God is your wing and won't let you fall. He's always there to catch you. (Psalm 37:24)

"The LORD himself watches over you! The LORD stands beside you as your protective shade." (Psalm 121:5)

THE LONG HAUL

____

____

____

____

____

____

____

DO YOU HAVE TIME TO TALK?

There's nothing wrong with opening up to someone when your heart is heavy. But you must be wise about whom you're sharing with. (1 John 4:1)

See, sometimes folks just want to hear your struggles to smile inside. When in actuality, they're smiling inside, gloating over your despair. (Matthew 7:15)

Remember, be careful that the friend with the quick listening ear isn't the enemy with the running mouth. (Proverbs 16:28)

"Their tongues sting like a snake; the venom of a viper drips from their lips." (Psalm 140:3)

THE LONG HAUL

STRIKE BACK

It's often a knee-jerk reaction when someone attacks you to strike back. But because you want to do it doesn't mean you should. (Hebrews 10:30)

See, as hard as you want them to hurt as they hurt you; it's just not for you to do. You must leave it for God to handle. (Romans 12:19)

Remember, don't become like the people that hurt you. (1 Samuel 24:12)

"For he is God's servant for your good. But if you do wrong, be afraid, for he does not bear the sword in vain. For he is the servant of God, an avenger who carries out God's wrath on the wrongdoer." (Romans 13:4)

THE LONG HAUL

____

____

____

____

____

____

____

IT WILL STOP

Heartbreak of any kind can hurt. But one thing is for sure; it will come to an end. (Psalm 34:18-20)

See, no matter what you're going through or how you feel. God knows about it, and as much as it hurts—it's working for your good. (Romans 8:28)

Remember, those tears will stop, and the pain will end. (Isaiah 60:20)

"He will wipe away every tear from their eyes, and death shall be no more, neither shall there be mourning, nor crying, nor pain anymore, for the former things have passed away." (Revelation 21:4)

THE LONG HAUL

THE UNDERRATED LANGUAGE

One of my favorite quotes comes from Lao Tzu, *"Silence is a source of great strength."* (Proverbs 17:28)

See, some folks can work your last nerve. And as much as you want to voice your concern. It's always best to remain silent. (Proverbs 29:11)

Remember, silence is an underrated language. LEARN IT! (Psalm 62:5)

"The tongue of the wise commends knowledge, but the mouth of the fool spouts folly." (Proverbs 15:2)

THE LONG HAUL

STILL DRINKING EXPIRED MILK?

If you've ever tasted expired milk, you know it's nasty and should be thrown out immediately. (James 4:7)

See, you have to know when to throw out the carton. In other words, what are you allowing in your life that has expired? (1 John 2:19)

It's a simple question: *Are YOU tired of drinking expired milk?* (Proverbs 26:11)

"Remember not former things and look not on things of old." (Isaiah 43:18)

THE LONG HAUL

POKING THE BEAR

As much as you want to respond to everything someone says—DON'T! (Proverbs 15:1)

See, some folks love poking the bear. So they will say anything to get you to growl. (James 1:19)

Remember, there's no need to respond to every comment. Some people aren't looking for answers. They're looking for an argument. (Proverbs 15:18)

"Sin is not ended by multiplying words, but the prudent hold their tongues." (Proverbs 10:19)

THE LONG HAUL

NO REGRETS

You will drive yourself crazy thinking of all the could and should have's in life. (Philippians 3:13-14)

See, never regret anything that has happened in your life. God allows everything for a reason. (Romans 8:28)

Remember, it happened. Therefore, it can't be changed or undone. So, learn from it and MOVE ON! (2 Corinthians 5:17)

"Do not call to mind the former things; pay no attention to the things of old." (Isaiah 43:18)

THE LONG HAUL

____

____

____

____

____

____

____

____

____

A HARDENED HEART

Life is all about lessons, and sometimes they will be hard. But you can't let them make your heart harden. (Psalm 51:10)

See, often, when you allow bitterness, rage, and resentment to soak in, it affects your heart. Making it cold. (Hebrews 12:15)

Remember, don't let a hard lesson harden your heart. (Proverbs 4:23)

"And I will give you a new heart, and a new spirit I will put within you. And I will remove the heart of stone from your flesh and give you a heart of flesh." (Ezekiel 36:26)

THE LONG HAUL

____

____

____

____

____

____

____

____

WHAT DID GOD SAY?

Sometimes folks only hear what they want. This means they focus on what others say and close their ears to God's voice. (John 8:47)

See, the enemy has a way of making you hear the naysayers. And once you listen to them, you forget the words of God. (1 John 4:6)

Remember, before you do anything, ask yourself: What did God say? (John 10:27)

"And your ears shall hear a word behind you, saying, 'This is the way, walk in it', when you turn to the right or when you turn to the left." (Isaiah 30:21)

THE LONG HAUL

DIFFERENT AGENDAS

Sometimes you ask God to heal what hurts, but God wants you to leave it alone. (Proverbs 19:21)

See, discernment is key. And God knows what's best. So even when you think you want it, God knows what's in your best interest. (Hebrews 5:14)

Remember, your agenda isn't the same as God's. (Psalm 33:10)

"We can make our own plans, but the LORD gives the right answer." (Proverbs 16:1)

THE LONG HAUL

____

____

____

____

____

____

____

____

SITTING ON THE TRACK

Have you ever seen someone begging a train attendant to wait because they think someone is still coming to join them? (Habakkuk 2:3)

See, at some point, the train has to leave. And no matter how long you want to wait, the conductor *(God)* is telling you it's time to go! (Jeremiah 29:11)

Remember, you will never get what God has in store if you wait for someone who isn't coming. (Isaiah 43:19)

"A time to seek, and a time to lose; a time to keep, and a time to cast away." (Ecclesiastes 3:6)

THE LONG HAUL

SIMILAR DYSFUNCTION

Sometimes what you think is comfort—isn't. (Proverbs 3:5–6) See, change is good. But often, folks are so comfortable with those "zones" that they become too fearful of leaping. (2 Timothy 1:7)

Remember, don't call it combability when it's similar to dysfunction. (Proverbs 13:20)

"Leave the presence of a fool, for there you do not meet words of knowledge. The wisdom of the prudent is to discern his way, but the folly of fools is deceiving." (Proverbs 14:7-8)

THE LONG HAUL

YOU CAN'T SEE HIM WORKING

Have you been praying or standing, yet—nothing is happening? (Psalm 27:14)

See, sometimes folks get agitated with God because they think He isn't working on their behalf. But that's not true. He works all things together for your good. (Romans 8:28)

Remember, just because you can't see Him working doesn't mean He isn't doing it behind the scenes. (Isaiah 45:15)

"There are different kinds of working, but in all of them and in everyone it is the same God at work." (1 Corinthians 12:6)

THE LONG HAUL

____

____

____

____

____

____

____

____

WHY ARE YOU WATCHING ME BURN?

If you saw something you cared about up in flames, wouldn't you put it out?

See, some folks' actions don't match their words. So, even though they keep telling you what you want to hear, they show you they can't do it. (Proverbs 27:6)

Remember, if you're on fire, who will be there to put you out? (Proverbs 18:24)

"When you pass through the waters, I will be with you; and through the rivers, they shall not overwhelm you; when you walk through fire you shall not be burned, and the flame shall not consume you. For I am the Lord your God, the Holy One of Israel, your Savior." (Isaiah 43:2-3)

THE LONG HAUL

____

____

____

____

____

____

____

JEALOUS OF ONE SLICE

Let's face it; some folks are rotted to the bone with envy. But that's not your problem at all. (Proverbs 14:30)

See, you can't downplay or cover up who you are because of someone else's jealousy. That's their issue. (James 3:16)

Remember, you can give folks a whole loaf—and they will still be jealous of your one slice. (Ecclesiastes 4:4)

"Therefore, as I live, declares the Lord God, I will deal with you according to the anger and envy that you showed because of your hatred against them. And I will make myself known among them, when I judge you." (Ezekiel 35:11)

THE LONG HAUL

PART-TIME

If you worked part-time, would you expect full-time benefits? (2 Thessalonians 3:10)

See, if you have faith, it must be activated all the time, not half. (Ephesians 2:8-9)

Remember, part-time faith won't get you full-time victory. (1 John 5:4)

"But without faith it is impossible to [walk with God and] please Him, for whoever comes [near] to God must [necessarily] believe that God exists and that He rewards those who [earnestly and diligently] seek Him." (Hebrews 11:6)

THE LONG HAUL

____

____

____

____

____

____

____

____

THIS YEAR I'M GOING TO...

How many of you are all set to make your resolutions? (2 Corinthians 5:17)

See, just like you were ready last year, you knew how your life would be. Why? Because you had plans. But so did God. (Jeremiah 29:11)

Remember, you can outline what you want—but God's purpose will succeed. (Proverbs 16:9)

"Many are the plans in a person's heart, but it is the LORD's purpose that prevails." (Proverbs 19:21)

THE LONG HAUL

____

____

____

____

____

____

____

____

FAKE NEWS

It's amazing how people know more about your business than you do—So they think. (Jeremiah 1:5)

See, some folks love to talk and spread "fake news." But just because they roll it out doesn't make it true. (Leviticus 19:16)

Remember, you don't have to acknowledge or reply to lies. (Psalm 5:6) (Proverbs 12:22)

"A false witness will not go unpunished, and he who breathes out lies will not escape." (Proverbs 19:5)

THE LONG HAUL

DECEMBER 8

HE HAD TO KILL IT

It can be frustrating when you don't understand what God is doing in your life, but you still have to trust Him. (Proverbs 3:5)

See, you're focused on the now, but God knows the later. So, even if you're hurting, it's for your good. (Psalm 121:7-8) (Romans 8:28)

Remember, often, God will kill a thing, so it doesn't kill you. (Job 13:15)

"For He wounds, but He also binds; He strikes, but His hands also heal." (Job 5:18)

THE LONG HAUL

THE FRUSTRATED SEASON

The climate seasons are spring, summer, fall, and winter. However, most folks reside in the *"Frustrated Season."* (Daniel 2:21)

See, just as the four seasons end, so does your frustration. In other words, God is at work. You just have to be patient. (Philippians 2:13) (Psalm 27:14)

Remember, stand still, be silent and watch the deliverance of the Lord. (Exodus 14:13-14)

"Be patient, then, brothers and sisters, until the Lord's coming. See how the farmer waits for the land to yield its valuable crop, patiently waiting for the autumn and spring rains." (James 5:7)

THE LONG HAUL

CAN YOU TALK?

Have you ever reached out to someone to talk? Yet—they never got back to you. (Psalm 34:15)

See, everybody is going through something. And even though they can't listen, *"someone"* is waiting to hear from you. (Psalm 34:17)

Remember, God is always there and ready for you to pour your heart out to Him. You just have to do it. (Isaiah 41:10-13)

"In my distress I called upon the Lord; to my God I cried for help. From His temple He heard my voice, and my cry to Him reached His ears." (Psalm 18:6)

THE LONG HAUL

HELL SENT

As much as you want everything to be Heaven sent, the devil sends things too. (Ephesians 6:16)

See, the enemy loves to try to destroy you. And what often seems like a blessing might be pure hell in disguise. (John 10:10)

Remember, be careful about asking God to bless what is hell sent. (1 Peter 5:8)

"That we be not overreached by Satan. For we are not ignorant of his devices." (2 Corinthians 2:11)

THE LONG HAUL

KEEP THE VOLUME DOWN

Some folks love to push your buttons. But just because they hit them doesn't mean you raise your voice. (James 3:6)

See, you have to refrain from anger. Therefore, you don't have to reply, just because they spoke. (Psalm 37:8)

Remember, being silent is the best response for a fool. (Proverbs 15:2, 23:9)

"Do not answer fools according to their folly, or you will be a fool yourself." (Proverbs 26:4)

THE LONG HAUL

THIS IS HOW YOU FEEL

If you've never been through something, how can you tell someone how they feel about what they're experiencing? (2 Timothy 3:12)

See, it's one thing to walk through the shoes of a person to guide them because you've been there before. But if you haven't—what advice are you giving? (Proverbs 12:15)

Remember, unless you've dealt with the same situation, be silent! (Proverbs 17:28)

"The righteous person faces many troubles, but the LORD comes to the rescue each time." (Psalm 34:19)

THE LONG HAUL

IT'S SACROSANCT

Would you allow someone to put something on you that would contaminate your body? (2 Corinthians 7:1)

See, the same way you protect your outer must be the same as the inner. And your mind will believe what you tell it. So, just because folks say something to you doesn't mean you let it soak in. (Romans 12:2)

Remember, your mind is sacrosanct—so guard it with your life! (Philippians 4:7)

"For the weapons of our warfare are not of the flesh but have divine power to destroy strongholds. We destroy arguments and every lofty opinion raised against the knowledge of God and take every thought captive to obey Christ." (2 Corinthians 10:4-5)

THE LONG HAUL

____

____

____

____

____

____

BLUE IN THE FACE

No matter how hard you try to explain yourself. Some folks are dead set on misinterpreting your words. (Proverbs 16:24)

See, you can talk until you're blue in the face. But if someone isn't ready to receive your words—you're speaking for nothing. (Colossians 4:6)

Remember, if you can't talk to them, talk to God. (Psalm 66:19)

"In my distress I called upon the LORD; I cried to my God for help. From His temple He heard my voice, and my cry for His help reached His ears." (Psalm 18:6)

THE LONG HAUL

REFILLED WITH PEACE

God doesn't give you a spirit of fear. That's a fact. So, if you know that, why are you filled with worry? (2 Timothy 1:7)

See, the enemy loves to attempt to destroy you, and it starts with lies. And once you believe it—you lose your faith in God. (John 8:44, 10:10)

Remember, it's time to release all fear and worry and refill your heart with God's peace. (Ephesians 6:10-18)

"Now, may the Lord of peace himself give you peace at all times and in every way. The Lord be with all of you." (2 Thessalonians 3:16)

THE LONG HAUL

THANK YOU, GOD

You can pray and ask God for what you desire, but that doesn't mean that's His plan for you. (Proverbs19:21) (Jeremiah 29:11)

See, as painful as it is—God knows what's best for you. So, even when it's killing you inside, it's for your good. (Romans 8:28)

Remember, stop questioning what He's doing. Instead, tell Him: THANK YOU! (Ephesians 5:20)

"The fear of the LORD leads to life, and whoever has it rests satisfied; he will not be visited by harm." (Proverbs 19:23)

THE LONG HAUL

GOOD TRY - BUT IT DIDN'T WORK

Throwing fiery darts is a trick of the enemy. But just because they get thrown doesn't mean they stick. (Ephesians 6:16) (Isaiah 54:17)

See, *enemies* intend to harm you. In other words, they mean it for evil. But God turns it around for your good. (Genesis 50:20)

Remember, they can try to break and destroy you—but it won't work! (Micah 7:8)

"We are hunted down, but never abandoned by God. We get knocked down, but we are not destroyed." (2 Corinthians 4:9)

THE LONG HAUL

ONLY 24 HOURS

I f you've never had a bad day—keep on living. (James 1:2-7) See, all days come to an end. So even if you think it's the worst day of your life, tomorrow is coming. (Psalm 30:5)

Remember, the bad day you're having is only 24 hours long. (2 Corinthians 5:17)

"In that day you will say: 'O LORD, I will praise You. Although You were angry with me, Your anger has turned away, and You have comforted me.'" (Isaiah 12:1)

THE LONG HAUL

RETURN IT

Just because you receive a package doesn't mean you have to open it. (1 Peter 5:8)

See, unfortunately, everything that comes to you is not sent with good intentions. This is why you must use discernment to determine good from evil. (Hebrews 5:14)

Remember, sometimes, you must use the label *"return to the sender"* for your peace. (Psalm 109:19 NLT)

"And a harvest of righteousness is sown in peace by those who make peace." (James 3:18)

THE LONG HAUL

____

____

____

____

____

____

____

____

CATCHING HELL

Let's face it; some folks love to see you catching hell. (Micah 7:8) See, just because you're going through despair, doesn't mean you have to give up. (2 Corinthians 4:8-9)

Remember, they can see you hurt, but never give them the satisfaction of letting them see you quit. (Galatians 6:9)

"But as for you, be strong and do not give up, for your work will be rewarded." (2 Chronicles 15:7)

THE LONG HAUL

BROKEN INTO PIECES

If someone broke you, do you think they would joyfully rush to pick up the pieces to put you back together? (Psalm 31:12,147:3)

I can answer for you—they won't! See, folks often want the one that caused the brokenness to admit it and fix it. But the fact is that's not going to happen. (Psalm 34:18)

Remember, despite what they did to cause the breakage. YOU must pick up your broken pieces to place them together. (Jeremiah 18:4)

"God, pick up the pieces. Put me back together again. You are my praise!" (Jeremiah 17:1) (MSG)

THE LONG HAUL

THE ACTIONS SPEAK

Folks will tell you anything—and will promise they mean it. But in the end, what they *do* speaks volumes. (James 2:18)

See, when you're a person of action, you showcase who you are. And it doesn't matter what you keep professing with your mouth. It's your character in what you do. (Proverbs 11:3)

So, ask yourself: *Are you a talker or a person of action?* (Matthew 5:37)

"This is what the Lord has commanded. If a man vows a vow to the Lord, or swears an oath to bind himself by a pledge, he shall not break his word. He shall do according to all that proceeds out of his mouth." (Numbers 30:1-2)

THE LONG HAUL

GOING UNDER THE KNIFE

If you had surgery, do you expect to get up from the operating table and run a marathon the next day? (James 5:15) The answer is simple, you might want to, but your body wouldn't allow you to. (3 John 1:2)

See, no matter what traumatic experience or hurt you've dealt with—it's like going under the knife. And as much as you want to rush your healing. The wound doesn't heal overnight. (Psalm 147:3)

Remember, stop fighting the process; it takes time to heal. (Jeremiah 33:6)

"For I will restore health to you, and your wounds I will heal, declares the Lord." (Jeremiah 30:17)

THE LONG HAUL

____

____

____

____

____

____

____

I CAN'T BUY PRESENTS

Christmas is a time of love, sharing, peace, and holiday cheer. But unfortunately, some folks aren't cheerful. (Proverbs 17:22)

See, sometimes folks get so caught up in the gifts and buying presents that they forget the presence of God and what today is actually about. (Psalm 16:11)

Remember, today; we celebrate Christ's birth—it's about Him! (Isaiah 9:6)

"For unto you is born this day in the city of David, a Savior, who is Christ the Lord." (Luke 2:11)

THE LONG HAUL

THE MAGICAL TWO WORDS

How many of you often say the magical two words to a common question: *"I'm Fine,"* All while suffering silently? (Romans 5:3-5; 8:18)

See, no one is exempt from adversity and affliction. Now, yours may differ from your neighbor's, but the trials you face still exist. (James 1:2-4)

Remember, you can lie to yourself and others to convey that you're fine. But God knows the truth. (Psalm 34:19; 139:1-18)

"He will wipe away every tear from their eyes, and death shall be no more, neither shall there be mourning, nor crying, nor pain anymore, for the former things have passed away." (Revelation 21:4)

THE LONG HAUL

____

____

____

____

____

____

____

YOU CAN STOP ROCKING NOW

Whether big or small, some folks will worry over every little thing. The question is, does that describe you? (Philippians 4:6-7)

See, if you're worrying, it's on YOU. Because either you're going to trust God or you're not. (Psalm 9:10)

Remember, God has you covered. So you can stop rocking back and forth now. (Hebrews 13:6)

"The LORD is with me; I will not be afraid." (Psalm 118:6)

THE LONG HAUL

THE STORM OF DESTRUCTION

Sometimes what you won't do, God has to come and assist you. (Psalm 121:7-8)

See, some folks can't stand storms. Why? Because they come through raging to wreak havoc and destruction. But without them, you wouldn't know that you could make it through them. (Mark 4:38-41)

Remember, the storm you're in isn't to destroy you—but to make you. (Psalm 107:29) (2 Corinthians 12:8-10)

"Mightier than the thunder of the great waters, mightier than the breakers of the sea— the LORD on high is mighty." (Psalm 93:4)

THE LONG HAUL

____

____

____

____

____

____

____

JUMP TO SAVE YOUR LIFE

If you are afraid of heights and are in a burning building, but the only way out is through a window onto a life net, could you do the jump? (Hebrews 11:1,6)

See, as scared as you may be, staying anywhere that will cause great harm will require you to leap. (2 Timothy 1:7)

So, take a breath, grab God's unchanging hand—and say goodbye. (Malachi 3:6)

"Remember not the former things, nor consider the things of old. For I am about to do something new. See, I have already begun! Do you not see it? I will make a pathway through the wilderness. I will create rivers in the dry wasteland." (Isaiah 43:18-19)

THE LONG HAUL

____

____

____

____

____

____

____

PERMANENT SPEAK

When trials have succumbed to you, rejoicing is the last thing you think about, but one of the first things you should do. (James 1:2-4)

See, the enemy wants to see you sweat. And if you fall for his schemes— you will begin to speak words over your situation that are not of God. (Ephesians 6:10-18)

Remember, don't speak permanent words of temporary trials. (Proverbs 18:21) (2 Corinthians 4:17)

"And after you have suffered for a little while, the God of all grace, who has called you to His eternal glory in Christ, will Himself restore you, secure you, strengthen you, and establish you." (1 Peter 5:10)

THE LONG HAUL

BE THE CRAZY ONE THEN

Good or bad—Folks will talk about you no matter what you do. (Leviticus 19:16)

See, when God tells you to act, you move! Despite what people think. (Micah 6:8)

Remember, who cares what the critics say? Even if it makes you look crazy. (Genesis 6:8-22)

"For such is the will of God, that by doing right you silence the ignorance of foolish people." (1 Peter 2:15)

THE LONG HAUL

____

____

____

____

____

____

____

____

____

ABOUT THE AUTHOR

Travasa Holloway is the owner of TNHB Inspirations. She is a Henderson, Kentucky, native and resides now in South Carolina. Ms. Holloway is the proud mother of twin sons, Ra'Mon (Ray) & Rod Holloway, and the grandmother of two granddaughters, Avaya & Kalani, and grandson Jamari Holloway. She has been in media/advertising for over 25 years.

Ms. Holloway began writing from a healing place, which later became a healing place for others. She reaches thousands of readers through her daily devotionals as TNHB Inspirations, and she continues to be invited to speak to share her inspirational journey with others throughout the country. It's her hope and prayer that no matter what you're going through, you will be in for The Long Haul and never let go of God's unchanging hand.

The Long Haul is Travasa's fourth published Devotional. Her other Devotionals are ***At The End Of The Day***, ***The Next Day***, and ***In The Morning***.

For speaking engagements and purchases,
you may contact the author at:

tnhb@tnhb-inspirations.com
www.tnhb-inspirations.com

www.ingramcontent.com/pod-product-compliance
Lightning Source LLC
Chambersburg PA
CBHW050455160726
48003CB00001B/22